GREY GARDENS

the musical

GREY GARDENS

the musical

The Complete Book and Lyrics of the Broadway Musical

BOOK BY DOUG WRIGHT

MUSIC BY SCOTT FRANKEL

LYRICS BY MICHAEL KORIE

Applause Theatre & Cinema Books · New York
An Imprint of Hal Leonard Corporation

Playwrights Horizons, Inc., New York City, produced the world premiere of Grey Gardens *off-Broadway on February 10, 2006. Originally produced on Broadway by East of Doheny, Staunch Entertainment, Randall L. Wreghitt/Mort Swinsky, Michael Alden, Edwin W. Schloss, in association with Playwrights Horizons.* Grey Gardens *was developed with the assistance of the Sundance Institute.*

Published in 2007 by Applause Theatre & Cinema Books
An Imprint of Hal Leonard Corporation
19 West 21st Street, New York, NY 10010

Printed in the United States of America

Book design by Lesley Kunikis
Photos by Joan Marcus

Library of Congress Cataloging-in-Publication Data is available upon request.

ISBN-10 1-55783-734-1
ISBN-978-1-55783-734-9

www.applausepub.com

NOTES FROM THE COMPOSER
By Scott Frankel

*"It's very difficult to keep the line between the past and the present.
You know what I mean? It's awfully difficult."*
—"LITTLE" EDIE BEALE

I first heard those lines in the mid-1990s. During those years, I
spent my summers in Provincetown, a beatific spot at the very tip of
Cape Cod. Among my friends there, *Grey Gardens* was something of a
cultural touchstone. The documentary is a beguiling brew of love, loss,
eccentricity, high style, and nonconformity that seemed to affect all
of us in a very personal way. People I knew would quote lines from the
film verbatim. Or even replicate some of Little Edie's more "creative"
costume choices. Seeing the film at midnight screenings, or on worn
videocassette copies, I was hooked.

It wasn't until the year 2000, however, that I had the notion to turn
Grey Gardens into a musical. Admittedly, it was an offbeat idea. I mean,
reclusive cat ladies living in a condemned, decaying twenty-eight room
mansion isn't exactly *Guys and Dolls*. And a documentary had never been
adapted into a stage musical before. Undaunted, I persevered. The
story of "Little" Edie Beale and her mother, Edith, seemed very much
a tale worth exploring. Each of them were frustrated performers—the
mother was a soprano, the daughter fancied herself a dancer—and the
fact that music was so terribly important to them seemed like it could
serve as an "engine" to drive the musical.

When I approached Albert Maysles, the legendary filmmaker who,
along with his late brother David, helmed the 1975 documentary, I
found out that I had competition. A French opera composer wanted to
use *Grey Gardens* as the basis for a contemporary opera! It was a setback,
but I was determined. My argument was a simple one: the music that
was central to the existence of these women was American popular song,
the standards of the '20s, '30s, and '40s. I call it the Great American
Songbook: the works of Kern, Porter, Berlin, Noel Coward, Rodgers
& Hart, and the Gershwins. Certainly a musical—employing popular
idioms rather than classical ones—would be truer to the essential
musical ethos of the Beales. Fortunately, Albert agreed.

Lyricist Michael Korie and I had written two musicals together, so I was eager to have him bring his keen intelligence, empathy, and brilliant wordplay to this project. For the book, or libretto, I approached my old college classmate Doug Wright, who had written such ambitious and dazzling plays as *Quills* and the award-winning *I Am My Own Wife*. I thought that Doug would have the perfect sensibility for translating *Grey Gardens* to the stage and I felt certain that he was most likely already an ardent fan of the film—and he was. So much so, in fact, that he turned me down flat! Doug felt that the documentary was a brilliant and true portrait, but that it hinged on the very notion of its verisimilitude. These women really existed—so to turn them into fictionalized characters was potentially doing them a disservice. Furthermore, he noted quite correctly that the documentary is more of a character study and less of a narrative-driven work. Was there enough event and plot to make it stage-worthy?

It was at this juncture that we hit upon the notion of creating a first act that was set in 1941, allowing us to see what life was like at Grey Gardens when the house was in its heyday. Because the question that hangs over the documentary is: How could this have happened to these women, especially given their education, wealth, social standing, and beauty? Perhaps by investigating the past, we—and the audience—could better understand where they ended up. It also would allow us, as authors, to flex our stylistic muscles by essaying a first act that had the froth and fun of *The Philadelphia Story* or *High Society,* but with darker underpinnings. Doug was now enthusiastically convinced we could make a go of it—and so we began to write. The three of us got our best work done outside of the frenzy of our New York City lives. We would go off on writing retreats—to Provincetown (where it all began), to the MacDowell Colony in New Hampshire, to the Berkshires, etc. The challenge was to somehow be true to the essence of the Beale women. Pulling us in sometimes opposing directions were concerns that we needed to make the musical work on its own terms, independent of the documentary—it had to connect with an audience of *Grey Gardens* neophytes. But we were also mindful of not homogenizing it for the legions of aficionados for whom any adaptation was borderline sacrilege. Along the way, Albert Maysles gave us wise counsel. "Remember," he said, "not to take sides. One is not the villain, the other the victim—it's more complicated than that. At the end of the day, it is really a mother-daughter love story."

In 2004, we had the marvelous opportunity to continue our development of the show with a workshop at the Sundance Institute at White Oak. In the extraordinary surroundings of an 8,000-acre nature preserve in northern Florida, we assembled an exemplary company of actors, most of whom are still in the cast, including our two brilliant leading ladies, Christine Ebersole and Mary Louise Wilson. With their input, and with the invaluable guiding hand of our masterful director, Michael Greif, we experimented, wrote, rewrote, and continued to refine the material. For me, as a composer, it was a particular thrill to be able to write music specifically for Christine. She is a composer's best friend and truly my muse. When we came back to New York, Tim Sanford, the artistic director of Playwrights Horizons, offered us a home to continue to work on the piece. More workshops and readings followed, finally culminating in an elaborate full production on the main stage at Playwrights in early 2006. The off-Broadway run was sold out and we were extended three times. Just before the final week of performances, the producer Kelly Gonda saw the show and bravely decided that she was going to move the show to Broadway. After additional rewrites, *Grey Gardens* began previews at the Walter Kerr in October, with an opening night on November 2, 2006. The Edies had arrived.

What is it about this story that so touches all of us? When the documentary came out, Jacqueline Onassis was the most famous woman in the world. So it must have been titillating to learn that she, too, had "unusual" family members hidden away, just like the rest of us. Of course, there was also a hefty dose of schadenfreude. "JACKIE'S KIN LIVING IN FILTH AND SQUALOR!" screamed the tabloids. Clearly, not even wealth, fame, and beauty could make one immune to life's mishaps and disappointments. But there's more to it than that. The story of the Beale women is a uniquely American one. Their fierce individuality, style, and intelligence remained a constant even as their world—and the world around them—changed. That they lived with such energy and joy is an inspiration ("Staunch women," as Edie put it). And in the end, they became cultural icons—not for their exceptional talent, but for being exceptionally true to themselves. With apologies to F. Scott Fitzgerald, not only are there second acts in American lives— there are third acts as well!

The themes explored in *Grey Gardens* are clearly universal ones that fascinate audiences: roads not taken, missed opportunities, love spiked with resentment, mental instability, reality vs. delusion. Any parent-child relationship is riddled with complicated, and sometimes contradictory, threads, mother-daughter ones all the more so.

Inside the house, things are not black and white, but literally "grey." For it is not only the story of this particular mother and daughter but also the story of the nation. In the 1970s, the Beales' house was a squalid eyesore in great disrepair while its inhabitants were steadfast and true. By contrast, the White House during the Nixon presidency had the outward appearance of propriety and beauty but was going to rot on the inside. Today, as then, we are a country engaged in an unpopular war, dependent on foreign oil, and governed by a leader who is increasingly out of touch. Is it any wonder that *Grey Gardens* still speaks to audiences today?

When Albert and his brother first screened the documentary for the ladies, Little Edie was reported to have said, "Well, I like it—but I really wish there was more singing and dancing." I like to think that we have made some kind of posthumous restitution to that end. Before Edie died in 2002, Albert Maysles wrote to her and proposed our idea to musicalize *Grey Gardens*. She replied:

Dearest Al—

I am thrilled by what you wrote about the musical 'G.G'! My whole life was music and song! It made up for everything! Thrilled-thrilled-thrilled! I have all of mother's sheet music and her songs that she sang! With all I didn't have, my life was joyous!

Love always,

Edie

P.S. It must be historical! My beloved mother! Edith Ewing Bouvier!

GREY GARDENS

the musical

GREY GARDENS—SONGS

PROLOGUE—1973

"The Girl Who Has Everything" .... Edith

ACT ONE—1941

"The Girl Who Has Everything" .... Edith
"The Five-Fifteen" .... Edith, Gould, Jackie, Lee, and Brooks
"It's Her" .... Edith, Gould, Edie, and Joe
"Mother Darling" .... Edie, Edith, and Gould
"Goin' Places" .... Joe and Edie
"Marry Well" .... Major Bouvier, Brooks, Jackie, Lee, and Edie
"Hominy Grits" .... Edith, Gould, Jackie, and Lee
"Two Peas in a Pod" .... Edie and Edith
"Drift Away" .... Gould and Edith
"The Five-Fifteen" [Reprise] .... Edith
"Daddy's Girl" .... Edie and Joe
"The Telegram" .... Edie
"Will You?" .... Edith

Intermission

ACT TWO—1973

"The Revolutionary Costume for Today" .... Edie
"The Cake I Had" .... Edith
"Entering Grey Gardens" .... Company
"The House We Live In" .... Edie and Company
"Jerry Likes My Corn" .... Edith and Edie
"Around the World" .... Edie
"Will You?" [Reprise] .... Edith and Edie
"Choose to Be Happy" .... Norman Vincent Peale and Company
"Around the World" [Reprise] .... Edie
"Another Winter in a Summer Town" .... Edie and Edith
"The Girl Who Has Everything" [Reprise] .... Edith and Edie

CHARACTERS
[in order of appearance]

PROLOGUE (1973)
Edith Bouvier Beale
"Little" Edie Beale

ACT ONE (1941)
Edith Bouvier Beale
"Little" Edie Beale
George Gould Strong
Brooks, Sr.
Jacqueline "Jackie" Bouvier
Lee Bouvier
Joseph Patrick Kennedy, Jr.
J. V. "Major" Bouvier

ACT TWO (1973)
Edith Bouvier Beale
"Little" Edie Beale
Brooks, Jr.
Jerry
Norman Vincent Peale

SETTING
Act One takes place in July 1941
Grey Gardens, East Hampton, Long Island, N.Y.

Intermission

Act Two takes place in 1973
Grey Gardens, East Hampton, Long Island, N.Y.

The events of the play are based on both fact and fiction.

PROLOGUE

1973

Grey Gardens, East Hampton, Long Island, NY

ACT ONE

July 1941

Grey Gardens, East Hampton, Long Island, NY

PROLOGUE: EXTERIOR OF GREY GARDENS—1973

(Underscoring: "GREY GARDENS")

(Over underscoring we hear a news report from a period television broadcast, grainy with static.)

NEWSCASTER

. . . In a statement released today, Jacqueline Kennedy Onassis confirmed that her eighty-year-old aunt, Mrs. Edith Bouvier Beale, and her adult daughter Edie are living in squalid conditions in an East Hampton estate known as Grey Gardens.

(Slowly, the lights rise on Grey Gardens, a moldering ruin hidden in the shadows of overgrown foliage. A series of 1970s newspaper articles appear projected upon the house.)

"MOTHER AND DAUGHTER ORDERED TO CLEAN HOUSE OR GET OUT"

"JACKIE'S AUNT TOLD: CLEAN UP MANSION"

"SADNESS OVER GREY GARDENS"

"JACKIE O'S RELATIVES LIVE AS RECLUSES IN RUIN"

NEWSCASTER

The house that once played host to Howard Hughes and the Rockefellers is now a refuge for fifty-two stray cats, a few rabid raccoons, and its two reclusive inhabitants, all living in an environment the Health Department calls "unfit for human habitation." Mrs. Onassis described the situation as a private family matter.

(Through the window we make out a woman sitting inside—Edith Bouvier Beale, a.k.a. "Big Edie," in a tattered housedress and enormous, floppy sun hat.)

And so we're left to ponder . . . how could American royalty fall so far, so fast?

(The tinny sound of a gramophone; the strains of an old, sentimental song. Edie cries out in victory.)

EDIE

I've found it, Mother darling! I found your old record!

(Edith listens to the scratchy old record, crooning along with the singer on the record . . . who happens to be herself, many years ago.)

(Song: "THE GIRL WHO HAS EVERYTHING")

RECORD

She is the girl
Who has everything.

EDITH

. . . Everything!

RECORD

She has the world on a string.

EDITH

. . . On a string!

("Little" Edie Beale appears in the window, in a broad-brimmed hat. She primps, looking at herself in a hand mirror.)

EDIE
(offstage)

Isn't it wonderful? God, aren't you just mad about this old tune?

EDITH

I recorded it in 1941. I was very serious about my singing; loved it.

(Edith begins out the front door.)

EDIE
(alarmed)

Mother darling, where are you going?

EDITH

Out on the porch. With the kitties. They just adore sun; you know how kitties are.

(Edith emerges on the sun-splashed porch. She addresses the audience.)

EDITH

We have some of the most beautiful kitties in the world! I just want to elope with 'em. Put 'em in a basket and elope with 'em.

EDIE

Mother, please! You mustn't show yourself like that! It annoys the neighbors.

EDITH

Oh, it does not . . .

EDIE

And the summer people! They roll down their car windows and snap Polaroids.

EDITH

I've got nothing to hide!

(Anxiously, Little Edie peers through binoculars to the street outside.)

EDIE

No! They've read about us, in the checkout line at the A&P. Our picture, right alongside Elizabeth Taylor's drinking problem.

EDITH
(a derisive snort)
Oh, Elizabeth Taylor! Here, kitty!

EDIE

They're calling us "cat ladies." And our house. They're saying Grey Gardens is a "public eyesore."

EDITH

Grey Gardens is one of the most renowned homes in America . . .
(sings along with the record)

She is the girl who has everything . . .

EDIE

Remember? You sang this song for me. I was "The Girl Who Had Everything" once.

EDITH

That's ancient history.

EDIE

(mournfully)

Yeah. Everything minus the ring.

EDITH

I don't think people should get married; I don't believe in it at all.

EDIE

If you can't get a man to propose to you, you might as well be dead.

EDITH

I'd take a dog over a man any day.

EDIE

You lived. I never lived.

EDITH

You liked your dancing; you were very good at that. And you had music all the time.

(Once again, Edith picks up the strains of the song.)

She is the girl who has everything . . .
Talent and beauty and sublime . . . !

(Suddenly, the great house creaks and splits. Time recedes, and we find ourselves in . . .)

SCENE 1—1: THE PARLOR & FOYER—1941

(. . . Grey Gardens on a balmy summer morning in late July 1941, the house's heyday. Its interior is tastefully furnished, a large, airy drawing room with French doors, which lead into a glass-walled solarium and beyond. Through an archway stands the foyer and the staircase leading to the second level. Looming above the quarried mantelpiece is an imposing portrait of Phelan Beale, distinguished, and, at age fifty, sporting jowls.

His wife, Edith Bouvier Beale, is a fiercely attractive woman sporting a royal blue Japanese kimono and a turban. She stands at a baby grand piano accompanied by George Gould Strong, a dapper fellow with pomaded hair and an ascot, a drink and a lit cigarette always nearby. Sitting on the ottoman is young Edie, gorgeous, long limbed, and in youth's prime. She listens dutifully to her mother croon.)

EDITH

. . . The crowds and the clamor
Aroused by her glamour
Will fade like the echo of a chime.
She's the girl who has everything . . .
But time.

(Edie jumps up, applauds to please them both.)

EDIE

Mother darling, what a *charming* song!

EDITH

The gift of music for your special day. Gould was up all night, composing!
> (with an approving look to Gould)

We've our very own maestro, haven't we, Edie?

EDIE

It's almost *too* much. Truly. Promise you won't perform it for *anyone* but me.

EDITH

Why, Edie, whatever do you mean?

(The telephone trills.)

EDIE

Well, it's awfully grand, isn't it? "The Girl Who Has Everything"?
Honestly! What would people think?

(Brooks, the African-American butler, enters, youthful with an
efficacious gait.)

BROOKS
(picking up the receiver)

Beale residence.
(to Edith)

Ma'am? The florist on the line.

EDITH

I'll take it in the kitchen. Come along, Gould. You'd best come with me
and get something to eat. Bloody Marys do not a breakfast make.

GOULD
(drolly)

Oh, is it morning?

(They exit.)

BROOKS

Congratulations, Miss Beale. It's not every day a young lady celebrates
her engagement.

EDIE

Brooks, please, tell the truth!
(with urgency)

At the party today . . . Mother's not planning to sing, is she?

BROOKS

Not if your father has a word to say about it.

EDIE

Remember my cotillion? When she stopped the party cold and performed all three arias from *Faust*?

BROOKS

Oh yes.

EDIE

Or my graduation tea! *Carmen,* with a rose in her teeth and a lace mantilla. And my birthday! When she danced *Salome,* and ruined all my Hermès scarves.
(a beat, and then . . .)
Wouldn't it be an odd thing, Brooks, if—on your death certificate—it actually said that you died of shame?

BROOKS

Would Mr. Kennedy like a breakfast tray in his room?

EDIE

Oh, for heaven's sake! I almost forgot! I promised him a walk to the beach.

(Edie swings open the French doors and takes in the garden, the sky.)

If life were a book, then today would mark a new chapter, wouldn't it? Out of Grey Gardens and into my own life.

(Reprise: "THE GIRL WHO HAS EVERYTHING")

. . . A guy to adore me,
A whole world before me.
The girl who has everything . . . is free.

(Edie sails out. Gould enters.)

GOULD

Brooks. I'd kill for a nice piece of fruit. Say . . . a lemon wedge or a twist of lime?

(Brooks hands him a ready drink.)

BROOKS

Your morning pick-me-up.

GOULD

You, sir, are a man of *boundless* compassion.

EDITH
(from offstage)

Brooks! Oh, Brooks!

(Edith reenters.)

I've had a harrowing chat with Mr. Gregory! He promised me roses, gardenias, and pansies; and now he says there isn't a pansy from Quogue to Shinnecock!

GOULD

He's lying; trust me.

EDITH

He's promised daisies instead; see that he stays true to his word.

BROOKS

You'll have them, ma'am. Now, about Mr. Beale; surely he's coming home for the party?

EDITH

I should say so! He's got to announce his daughter's engagement! Wall Street will have to do without him for one day!

(Song: "THE FIVE-FIFTEEN")

Mister Beale thinks making money matters more
Than a restful family summer by the shore.
But unless some act of God divine
Derails the New York—Montauk line,
He's arriving on the five-fifteen.

BROOKS

Then I'll have the car waiting at the station—

(Brooks exits. Edith glances about surreptitiously to ensure the coast is clear.)

EDITH

Well?

(Gould passes her a page from atop the piano, a printed recital program.)

Why it's gorgeous! Look how handsomely it's typeset!
(reads it aloud)
"A musical recital in honor of Miss Edith Bouvier Beale and Mr. Joseph Patrick Kennedy, Jr., the twelfth of July, 1941." Won't Edie be tickled pink?

GOULD

Oh, she'll be *stunned.*

(The French doors fling open. In run two little girls. Jackie, twelve, is in a petite riding outfit, complete with a crop; Lee, eight, the tomboy, is dressed in overalls. They jostle and squeal.)

LEE

It's not fair! Jackie won't let me ride her stupid horse!

JACKIE

But, Aunt Edith, she's too young! Her feet don't reach the stirrups, and she can't even canter—

EDITH

Jacqueline Bouvier, where have you been? Saratoga! And Lee! Why, you're a *tribute* to dirt!

(Jackie sees Gould readying sheet music.)

JACKIE
(to Edith)
You're going to sing today, aren't you?

EDITH
Make yourselves useful; run out to the garden, and make some pretty little nosegays for the party—

JACKIE
Sing for us now!

LEE
Please!

EDITH
(any willing audience is a good audience)
Oh, for heaven's sake. Gould, what's first on the bill? "Indian Love Call"?

GOULD
(consults the recital program)
No, the mysterious Orient!

EDITH
Hit it!

(Song: "ITTY-BITTY GEISHA")

EDITH

Pretty itty-bitty geisha,
Delicate and small and sweet.
Kneeling on tatami,
Making origami,
Hobbling on her poor bound feet.

(The girls join in with her.)

	JACKIE and LEE
	Ooo! Eeoww!
EDITH	*Chimmy-chimmy-chow-chew!*
Pity itty-bitty geisha.	*Hoo-chee koo-chee koo!*
Hiding all her foolish pride . . .	

EDITH
Let your auntie Edith
Practice her recital.
Take your silly selves outside.

Scoot!

(The girls run outside to play, giggling.)

EDITH
Utter terrors, those two!

GOULD
I just adore children. Especially grown ones.

BROOKS
(reentering)
Ma'am. The caterer's arrived. Where'd you like him to set up—?

EDITH
Put the chafing dishes on the garden ledge
Once the gardener has finished with the hedge.
Chill the vichyssoise and heat the veal—
        (glances at portrait over the mantel)
And wish me luck 'cuz Mister Beale
Is arriving on the five-fifteen.

(Brooks exits to do her bidding.)

EDITH
What time is it?

GOULD
Half past eleven.

EDITH
Good Lord!
        (consults a list in her kimono pocket)

EDITH

One o'clock.
Set the chairs and the tables.
Two o'clock.
Raise the big white tent.
Three o'clock.
Reginaldo does our hair.

GOULD

Now *that* sounds promising.

EDITH

Four o'clock.
Hang the Japanese lanterns.
Five o'clock.
Mix the champagne punch.

(The girls bound back in with freshly plucked flowers for nosegays.)

JACKIE and LEE

Pick the inchworms off the peonies.

GOULD

Pink umbrellas for the daiquiris.

EDITH

The Ambassador and Rose will tour the grounds.
                    (imitates Rose Kennedy's manner)
"Like a spread from House & Garden, *" she expounds.*

GOULD

How nouveau riche.

EDITH

Have the piano tuned and moved outdoors
By cocktail hour—mine, not yours,
And restrict yourself to grenadine.

JACKIE and LEE

Nyah, nyah.

EDITH

You cannot be sloshed at five-fifteen.

(The phone rings. Brooks answers.)

BROOKS

Beale residence, hold please.
                              (to Edith)
Lady from *The Hamptons Bee.*

EDITH
                          (into phone)
Why, hello, Margaret! That's right, half past five. Oh, everyone, simply
le tout Park Avenue and la crème de Hyannis! Well, the press table's
going to be awfully crowded . . . but if you don't mind sharing a folding
chair with *Harper's Bazaar* . . . Sing? Me? Heavens no, it's Edie's day, not
mine . . . of course, people can be so insistent and I hate to disappoint.
Twist my arm, blackmail me, threaten my very life, and who knows? You
might get a verse of something . . . Yes, darling, half past!
                          (hangs up, asks all)
Where were we?

GOULD/BROOKS/JACKIE/LEE

One o'clock.

EDITH

Stake the droopy hydrangeas.

GOULD/BROOKS/JACKIE/LEE

Two o'clock.

EDITH

Fill the lotus pond.

GOULD/BROOKS/JACKIE/LEE

Three o'clock.

EDITH

Lock the cat up in its room.

JACKIE and LEE

Aw, poor kitty!

GOULD/BROOKS/JACKIE/LEE

Four o'clock.

EDITH

Glaze the salmon in aspic.

GOULD/BROOKS/JACKIE/LEE

Five o'clock.

EDITH

Crack the crab on ice.
With the privet pruned and manicured,
And my daughter's future well assured . . .
Grey Gardens will be decked out in its prime!

GOULD

Bright as a liberty dime!

EDITH

Little Edie will be here with Joe in time!

BROOKS

Hear them chapel bells chime!

EDITH

Like a Norman Rockwell family,
Our photo in The Hamptons Bee!

GOULD

The event of 1941!

JACKIE and LEE

Of East, West, South, and Bridge Hampton!

EDITH

(glances at portrait of Phelan Beale)
Though perhaps I've overspent a bit,
The man who's gonna pay for it—

EDITH/BROOKS/GOULD/JACKIE/LEE

Is arriving on the five-fifteen!

(Edith collapses onto the sofa together with her highly entertained nieces.)

BROOKS

Now about those daisies . . .

EDITH

What would we ever do without you, Brooks . . . ?

(As Brooks exits through one door, Edie sails in with her intended, Joseph Kennedy, Jr., a Greek god in beachwear, and charming to boot.)

EDIE

What a beautiful ocean it is today! A sort of sapphire.

(To herald the arrival of the girl of the moment, Gould plays a fawning flourish on the piano.)

(Song: "IT'S HER!")

GOULD

Bum-ba-da-da-da-da-dum!
It's her!
The darling of the day.
That pearl of the South Fork,
The apple of New York;
That carefree descendant
Of beauty resplendent,
And "born-to-the-manor" caché . . .

JOE

And look who whisked her away.
(greets Edith)
Mrs. Beale, I can't thank you enough. This is my first engagement party.

EDIE

And his last!
(a playful slap)
You're an absolute beast—

JOE

(taking Edie's hand)
I'm just crazy about Edie, and she knows it.
(back to Edith)
And my parents are awful keen to meet you.

EDITH

Likewise, I'm sure. Edie had such a splendid Fourth of July up at the
Cape; we're so pleased you could visit us here at our own little beach
cottage. I'd like you to meet my pianist, Mr. George Gould Strong.

(Gould rises to shake Joe's hand.)

GOULD

Somewhere in Athens, there's a pedestal missing its statue.

(Joe looks at him with evident disapproval.)

JOE

You're here to play for the party?

GOULD

I'm afraid I'm a permanent fixture, a grim inevitability. I fall
somewhere between death and taxes.

EDITH

Gould! You're a member of the family.

EDIE
(teasing)
It's true; we didn't have a black sheep of our own, so we had to import one. Isn't that right, Gould?

(Gould offers Edie a chilling smile. Edie notices the recital brochure atop the piano.)

EDIE
Why, Mother darling, what's this?

EDITH
Oh dear. You weren't supposed to see that. It was meant to be a surprise—

EDIE
(reading song titles with distaste)
"Itty-Bitty Geisha"? "Toyland"? "Gypsy Pasodoble"?

EDITH
Just a few popular favorites.

EDIE
You're planning to *sing*?

EDITH
It's not a party without music.

EDIE
But, Mother darling—

EDITH
Gould and I have been slaving away like a couple of Phoenicians.

EDIE
(counting the number of songs)
One, two, three, four, five, six, seven, eight . . . nine?

Not counting encores.

(Song: "MOTHER DARLING")

EDIE

Mother darling . . .
Dearest mother darling . . .
I am honored more than I can say
By this wondrous . . . truly . . .
Verging on unduly
Heartfelt motherly display.
And you know how much I love your singing
As I've said so many times before.
Every Christmastime . . .
Every christening . . .
Every time that you sing
I'm first to shout "encore,"
But . . .
Mother darling,
Let a daughter have her day!
It's a day for me . . .
And all of us to shine.
Though your "Apache Maiden Serenade" is too divine,
The parents of the groom
Are just a wee bit formal.
Help them think that we are normal.
Mother darling,
Sing a little song—not nine.

EDITH

"How sharper than a serpent's tooth . . ."

EDIE

Please, Mother darling—

EDITH

Who knows if we'll ever have another party? Everyone leaving; why, it's your mother's swan song!

EDIE

It's just that Joe's parents are coming, and they're so terribly New England, aren't they, Joe? I don't expect they listen to music at all. Just hymns and military marches.

JOE

Nonsense. I'm sure they'd be delighted—

EDIE

Joe. Please. You mustn't encourage her.

JOE

Besides, she has a beautiful voice—

EDIE

I mean it.

EDITH

Edie, pumpkin . . .
Mama's precious treasure . . .
I am slightly mystified to learn
Of your sudden . . . urgent . . .
Dare I say insurgent
Dearth of daughterly concern.

EDIE

But . . .

EDITH

For you know how Gould and I adore you—

EDIE

Yes . . .

EDITH

And rehearsed for weeks on your behalf.

(Edie reads from the recital program.)

EDIE

Madame Butterfly. Tosca's aria.

EDITH

It's my best.

EDIE

Let it rest. I'll just die if people laugh!

EDITH

Laugh?

EDIE

Decorum, Mother, that's all I
ask! The best singers—the real
professionals all know when to cede
the stage! When she doesn't
get exactly what she wants, she
positively *spits* venom! It's true!
Pish posh, Mother! You'll say
anything to be *dramatic,* anything to
garner *attention*—

EDITH

Decorum? Oh, that's rich!
You're a fine one to lecture
me about propriety! Those
visits from the headmistress!
Imagine! Wearing lipstick to
school—"temptation red!"—at
only thirteen; the whole town
was talking! Why this house—
this very house—was positively
blanketed in adolescent shame!

GOULD

Ladies—

EDITH

Gould—

EDIE

Mother—

GOULD

Please!

EDITH and EDIE

Let me get one word in!

GOULD

I'm surprised by both of you today—

EDITH

Both of you are way out of line.

GOULD

And this bossy, bratty—

EDITH and EDIE

Bratty?

GOULD

Bordering on catty, most unladylike melee.

EDIE

Whose engagement is this, anyway?

GOULD and EDITH

After months and months of preparation—

GOULD

You would think the program was resolved.

EDITH

So ungrateful!

EDIE
(tosses sheet music off the piano)
"Turkish Rhapsody."

EDITH

Not the rhapsody!

EDIE

"Venice Barcarolle."

EDITH

Not my barcarolle!

EDIE

This is out of control!

(to Joe)

Tell her, dear.

JOE

Don't get me involved here.

EDIE

Mother darling—

EDITH

Edie sweetheart—

GOULD

Talking to the wall . . .

EDIE

Let's let Daddy referee.

EDITH

Darling Daddy, where is he?

GOULD

Not where he should be.

(All take a deep breath, put on forced smiles.)

ALL

It's a day for me and all of us to shine!

GOULD

Might I suggest a compromise
Is very much in line.

EDIE

With moonlight on the waves,
Delphiniums in flower . . .
Save Puccini for the shower.

EDITH

Edie, angel.
Mother will sing eight . . . not nine.

EDIE
(concedes with resignation)

Fine.

EDITH

Fine?

GOULD

Fine.

EDITH/EDIE/GOULD

Fine.

(From offstage, the sound of shattering glass.)

BROOKS
(offstage)

Fore!

EDITH
(rushes to the window, peers out)

Oh, dear God!

JOE

What on earth was that?

EDITH

My father. The Major. Driving golf balls right into the solarium!
Brooks!

BROOKS
(reappears)

Ma'am?

EDITH

Brooks, shouldn't you be getting Papa dressed—or something—*anything*—

BROOKS

It's in progress, ma'am. Dinner jacket's all laid out; and I'll get the glass works on the line.

EDITH

Oh, thank you!

(And Brooks sails out again. Edith regards her daughter for a moment, then defiantly bursts *a cappella* into an operatic aria.)

EDITH

  O mio babino, caro . . . !

(She climbs the stairs, leaving silken notes in her wake. Edie rolls her eyes. A world-weary Gould raises his flask to Joe.)

GOULD

Here's to love . . . in all its infinite varieties.

(He tips his whiskey and ducks out. Edie turns to Jackie and Lee.)

EDIE

You two must find all this grown-up talk so dreadfully boring!

JACKIE and LEE

Nooo . . .

EDIE

You do so! Now scoot!

(Jackie and Lee sigh. Jackie approaches Joe and curtsies.)

JACKIE

Lovely to meet you, Mr. Kennedy.

JOE

Why, thanks, Jackie.

(Lee giggles. The two girls dash out. Joe turns back to Edie.)

JOE

That kid's got poise to spare, hasn't she?

EDIE

(still fuming)

Mother chose the florist! The decorations! And now this latest development . . . a concert! Honestly, Joe, I'm *slaughtered* by it!

JOE

Shh. Relax. What say we take some air?

(To calm her rising hysteria, Joe takes Edie by the arm and guides her outside to the garden.)

SCENE 1—2: PORCH, EXTERIOR

(Joe surveys the lavish grounds and garden.)

JOE

You'd really give all this up for me, Edie?

EDIE

Absolutely. It's like the poem . . . the one by Mr. Robert Frost? "Two roads diverged in a yellow wood . . ." Well, Mother took one path, Joe, and it led her here, to East Hampton. Me . . . why, I've simply *got* to take another.

JOE

Where would it lead, pray tell?

EDIE

Now don't laugh. Maybe to a Broadway stage . . . or the motion pictures!

JOE

And not to Washington, D.C.?

EDIE

Why, sure. If that's what you'd like.

JOE

I've got the perfect house in mind. Right on Pennsylvania Avenue.

(Song: "GOIN' PLACES")

Me and the old man mapped it out.
Fastest road to the Senate floor.
Youngest man to be senator-elect.

EDIE

How so?

JOE

The usual way.

> *Pick up some medals overseas.*
> *Kick the butts of those SOBs,*
> *Zip back home, get married, and gain respect.*

I'll fly back here to East Hampton, and I'll scoop you right up into the cockpit—

EDIE

My goodness, my hair!

JOE

> *Kid, we're goin' places.*
> *Goin' places*
> *Ya' never dreamed you'd see*
> *As your social graces*
> *Give some panache to me.*

EDIE

I'll do my best!

JOE

> *With your pensive smile*
> *And fearless style,*
> *That debonair joie de vivre—*
> *Kid, we're goin' places*
> *Your mama won't believe!*

EDIE

You know the trouble with the White House, Joe? It could use a little color!

> *Picture the White House I restore.*
> *Not to criticize Eleanor,*
> *Home decor just isn't her stock in trade.*

JOE

You dress up any room just by being in it.

EDIE
(tickled pink)

Oh, you!

And as a former Waldorf "deb"
I'll make fashion my cause célèbre.
Call it my American Style crusade!

Remember, Joe, it's not what you wear—

JOE

Oh no?

EDIE

It's how you wear it!

EDIE and JOE

Kid, we're goin' places.
Goin' places
We never dreamed we'd get.

JOE

As our love's embraces
Fill up the basinet.

EDIE
(laughs)

Slow down, not yet!

With your Colgate grin—
Dick Tracy chin—
That Hollywood film-star sheen—

BOTH

Kid, we're goin' places
The nation's never seen!

BOTH

New worlds await
Beyond the garden gate.

JOE

As long as we've each other—

EDIE

Long as I escape my mother!

JOE

Your mother? Shouldn't I be the one who matters most?

EDIE

Oh, but you are. Of course you are.

JOE

The way you talk, a fella could forget.

(To appease him, she pulls him into a kiss.)

EDIE

You're the only one on my dance card, Joe.

(They dance joyously.)

BOTH

All the signs are good,
So knock on wood
We're gonna be a-okay . . .
'Cuz the place we're goin',
We're goin' all the way . . . !
We're goin' all the way . . . !
We're goin' all the way . . . !

JOE

We're goin' all the way . . . !

(They embrace on the garden bench.)

SCENE 1—3: LAWN OF GREY GARDENS

(On the apron of the stage—bathed in the preternatural green of the well-tended lawn of Grey Gardens—Edith's father, Major Bouvier, wears a golf outfit and matching hat topped by a pompon. He is a lion-like scion of business in his early seventies. Around his neck hangs an ear trumpet. Brooks stands by with a bag of golf clubs slung over his shoulder as he waits impatiently for Major to finish golfing so that he can be ushered inside to change. Jackie and Lee sit on the sidelines, watching. Major swings. Brooks covers his eyes.)

MAJOR BOUVIER

Goddamn it, Brooks! Tee me up another, will you? One more swing to strengthen my nerve!

BROOKS

But, Major Bouvier, sir, the time—

MAJOR BOUVIER

Bother the time! The blasted party can't begin until Phelan arrives on the five-fifteen, can it?

JACKIE

But Edie's hoping for your blessing, Grandfather!

MAJOR BOUVIER

And have it she shall! Thank heavens she's hoodwinked this nice young Navy pilot.
                    (to Jackie and Lee, ominously)
Forgive me, ladies, but we live in perilous times.

JACKIE
                    (gravely)

The war, Grandfather?

MAJOR BOUVIER

The Jitterbug! Nylon stockings. Chantilly perfume. If you want to anchor yourself in an uncertain world . . . you've only one recourse!

(To a military-flavored march, Major steadies himself for a long golf drive.)

(Song: "MARRY WELL")

MAJOR BOUVIER

With your eye on the ball
And your feet on the fairway,
Hit it high, little girls—marry well.

(He swings. We hear the crack of the ball.)

BROOKS

Fore!

MAJOR BOUVIER

Every point under par
Is a leg up the stairway
To the sky, little girls—marry well.
Find a staunch young patrician
Republican,
With the blood and the brains to excel . . .
                        (indicates himself)
. . . Like the fine strapping lad
Your late grandmama had . . .
Meaning I, little girls—marry well.

BROOKS

I think, sir, you had best be going inside—

MAJOR BOUVIER

Inside where?

BROOKS

Grey Gardens, of course—

MAJOR BOUVIER

That madhouse? That Bohemia? That veritable museum of perversity,
a haven for misfits, Communists, and unpublished poets? Where that
no-good daughter of mine warbles like a loon, while that unsavory wisp
of a fella in a silk cravat tickles the ivories with fingers as soft and pale as
a ten-dollar whore?

BROOKS

That'd be the place, yes.

MAJOR BOUVIER

Ridiculous woman, Edith, flying in the face of every good solid value I
ever tried to instill in her. God knows, I tried to teach her, teach all of
my brood—

(Edie enters, overlapping him.)

MAJOR and EDIE

The hallmark of aristocracy is responsibility!

(Major Bouvier embraces Edie.)

MAJOR BOUVIER

Edie . . . the last hope of the great Bouvier clan!

EDIE
(fondly)

Oh, honestly—

BROOKS
(clears his throat)

Now, sir—

MAJOR BOUVIER

All right, all right, I'm coming. Company—fall in! Ten-hut!

EDIE

Chair the ball for the blind.

LEE

Treat your church to a steeple.

ALL

Well-endowed little girls marry well.

EDIE

Bail the Met out of debt.

JACKIE

Leave your art to the people.

ALL

And the crowd will fall under your spell.

MAJOR BOUVIER

But an unmarried lassie
Who's fast and loose
Is a moose in a herd of gazelle.

(Takes aim with his golf club, like a rifle.)

ALL

Pow!

MAJOR BOUVIER

Don't be picked off the pack
With your head on a plaque.
Do me proud, little girls.

ALL

Marry well.

MAJOR BOUVIER

Bear in mind, it's your future that counts. They say greatness always skips a generation. Well, now it's up to you to burnish the family crest.

MAJOR BOUVIER
(shows them the crest on his pocket watch)
Take a good look at it, children, and remember . . .

This crest of our French royal provenance—
It took a while for it.
We paid a pile for it.
So don't end up spinsters and dilettantes.
The name Bouvier will surpass all others.
All of your uncles, dads . . .

(He winces at a distant trill from Edith.)

. . . And mothers.

JACKIE
Our mother won't be a Bouvier at all, once her divorce is final!

LEE
She'll be what they call a "fallen woman"!

JACKIE
Sister Bridget says girls who come from broken homes wind up old maids, or worse.

LEE
What could be worse?

MAJOR
Winding up a nun, like Sister Bridget!

LEE
Picture Lee in Milan
With a prince and a villa!

MAJOR
Sally forth, little girl—very nice.

JACKIE

Jackie B. in Paree,
Simply bathed in chinchilla!

EDIE

As for me, Joe will more than suffice.

MAJOR

Good girl!

With a grandfather's blessing, I wish you love.
Someone there when your hair goes to grey . . .
And I'll strut in my spats
Down the aisle of Saint Pat's.

BROOKS

Marry high.

EDIE

Marry proud.

JACKIE and LEE

Nouveau riche ain't allowed.

BROOKS

Upper class.

EDIE and JACKIE

Upper crust.

LEE

Standard Oil and Morgan Trust!

EDIE

Marry young.

BROOKS

Marry chaste.

MAJOR BOUVIER

Or if not, then in haste.

ALL

Marry well
And you're well on your way!

(The Major triumphantly marches the Bouvier girls offstage.)

SCENE 1—4: THE PARLOR and FOYER

(Entering the foyer, Major Bouvier and the girls stop dead in their tracks as, in the parlor, Edith rehearses an egregious recital selection with Gould. Her soprano voice is ill suited to the Jolson-style number she's doing, dialect and all, immune to its inappropriateness.)

GOULD

Remember, you're an old-time mammy! Poor as dirt, true, but rich in the wisdom of the ages!

(Song: "HOMINY GRITS")

EDITH

Down in Carolina
Be ole black Dinah
Sweatin' and a-toilin' at da boilin' pot.
Stirrin' and a-scrapin'
Da steam escapin',
Cookin' up a breakfast dat hit da spot
'Cuz . . .
All God's chillun love hominy!
Hominy!
All God's chillun love hominy grits!
Fills to satiation
Da whole plantation!
Dem's da bestest vittles us colored folk gits!

(Major Bouvier and Edie are utterly appalled, particularly in front of Brooks.)

MAJOR BOUVIER

What the hell is she singing?

BROOKS
(drily)

Just one of her "freedom songs," sir.

EDITH

Sammy stir da kettle
So none don't settle.
Mulie heat da metal wit de kindlin' wood.
Once ya done your pickin'
Ya' git fried chicken.
Gotta start da day off wid somethin' good
'Cuz . . .

(Gould and the girls join in, to Major's distress.)

EDITH/GOULD

All God's chillun love hominy!
Hominy!
All God's chillun love hominy grits!

EDITH

Next to watermelon,
Dere ain't no tellin'
Dem's da bestest vittles—

EDITH/GOULD/JACKIE/LEE

Us colored folk gits!

MAJOR BOUVIER

Her mother was a quiet woman! Asthmatic! Demure!

(Edith does an absurd "shimmy" dance. The girls join the dance with exuberance. Major attempts to stop them, to no avail. Brooks watches with a blank expression.)

MAJOR BOUVIER

No! Not you, too!

GOULD

Go, girl! Stir dat kettle!

EDITH
(wiggling her behind)

Mmm-hmm!

GOULD

That'll do it—add some suet.

EDITH

Sho' 'nuff, boss—nuthin' to it.

MAJOR BOUVIER
(mortified, to Brooks)
If she were a whole horse instead of just its ass, I'd shoot her!
(to Edith)
You're a pernicious influence on the young and impressionable!

(Major Bouvier chases the girls around the living room, but they elude
him, ducking under the piano. In desperation, the Major slams the
piano lid down on Gould's fingers.)

GOULD

OW!!

MAJOR BOUVIER

That's enough! We've a guest in the house!

EDITH

It just so happens, Papa, that Mr. Kennedy holds music in the
utmost esteem.

MAJOR BOUVIER

All the more reason why he should be spared your caterwaul!

(Edie passes Major Bouvier her mother's recital program, spilling
the beans.)

EDIE

Mother's just rehearsing for this afternoon—

MAJOR BOUVIER
(noting program with dismay)

Goddamn it, Edith!
(to Jackie and Lee)

Upstairs, girls! I'd like a word alone with your aunt.

JACKIE

Everybody always—

LEE

Not again—

MAJOR BOUVIER

You heard me! Double-time!

(Disappointed, Jackie and Lee trundle upstairs. As Brooks exits, the
Major gives him a discreet nod. Ever obliging, Brooks closes the door
behind him.)

MAJOR BOUVIER

Last spring, she brings home that Getty fella. One aria and two medleys
later, he's heading for the hills with cotton in his ears.

EDIE
(to Edith)

It's true; you know it is—

MAJOR BOUVIER

Quiet! This is between your mother and me.

(Quelled, Edie blushes, stares at her lap.)

Edith, let's face it: you drive her suitors away faster than a social disease.

EDITH

Oh, it's *my* fault, is it?

MAJOR BOUVIER

Your outlandish behavior—

EDITH

My behavior? You remember what Father O'Hanlon said about
Little Edie, don't you? What the priest in school telephoned me *at
home* to say—

EDIE

For heaven's sake, I'm here! I'm in the room!

MAJOR BOUVIER

Edie's a spirited girl, that's all—

EDITH

"Spirited!" What a darling euphemism!

EDIE

Mother, please—

EDITH

Boys are "spirited!" Girls—well, I'm afraid the word's a bit bluer.

EDIE
(to Edith)

How dare you —

(to Major Bouvier)

How dare she—

MAJOR BOUVIER
(definitively)

Quiet, the both of you! Soon, you'll be miles apart. And better for it!
(to Edie)

You'll have a rich husband. You won't have to rely on your mother's
money . . .
(to Edith)

. . . And you'll have an empty nest. You won't have to rely on mine!
That trust fund you squander? Sayonara! I can put it all into war bonds,
where it belongs!

EDITH

Fine. From now on, Phelan will handle all of our financial affairs.

MAJOR BOUVIER

The "affairs" Phelan handles are strictly his own.

EDITH

That's not true!

MAJOR BOUVIER

Face facts, woman! There's a reason he keeps an apartment in the city.

EDITH

It's for business!

MAJOR BOUVIER

Of the monkey variety!

EDITH

We've a marvelous marriage! Perfectly marvelous! We've different interests, that's all. He has Wall Street and I have my music, and the companionship of Mr. George Gould Strong—

MAJOR BOUVIER

It's a disgrace, that's what it is—

EDITH

Gould here happens to be a boogie-woogie composer with the most terrific style. He's the most brilliant man I've ever met, including Mr. Beale and including you! He's completely brilliant!

MAJOR BOUVIER

How much does this brilliant fella eat?

GOULD
(meekly)

Just enough bread to sop up the gin—

MAJOR BOUVIER

And his cufflinks—who paid for those, I'd like to know?

EDITH

This is degrading, Daddy, it's simply shameful—

MAJOR BOUVIER

Yes! I'll hazard it is!

EDITH

You've nothing but contempt for me, have you?

MAJOR BOUVIER

(raising his ear trumpet)

Hmm? What was that?

(Suddenly, savagely, Edith grabs the ear trumpet and shouts into it.)

EDITH

I'm your daughter! Why must you hate me so?

(Major Bouvier pauses. He draws himself up to his full stature.)

MAJOR BOUVIER

Your mother and I reared you to be a lady, Edith Bouvier Beale. And what have you become instead? That most pitiable of creatures . . . an actress without a stage.

(Edith stares at him, hollow-faced, ashen.)

And now if you'll excuse me, I'm due for a shave. There's a party this afternoon, I'm told, and I'm hell-bent on making an honorable impression.

(Slowly, deliberately, he tears up the program. He hands it to Edith.)

I trust you'll do the same.

(With that, he stalks out of the room. Edith's face is impassive for a moment, stoic. Then it cracks in a torrent of tears. Gould breaks the silence by remarking to Edie in a low voice.)

GOULD

Satisfied?

(Edie ignores him, and turns to Edith.)

EDIE
(regretfully)

Mother, I—

EDITH
(not looking at her)

Don't.

EDIE

But—

EDITH

No.

(Edie looks to Gould; what should she do? Gould strands her with a shrug. But Edie has an idea; takes note of the music on the piano.)

EDIE

Oh my goodness, Gould. Is this on the bill? It's one of my favorites.

(Edie starts to sing, tenderly.)

> *Given our amazing similarities*
> *We could be a—*

EDITH
(interrupting)

Edie. Please.

EDIE

It's the very first song you ever taught me. We used to sing it together.

(She nods at Gould to accompany. He complies.)

(Song: "TWO PEAS IN A POD")

EDIE

Given our amazing similarities
We could be a plate of eggs and ham.
A pair of canaries,
I shadow you like Mary's lamb.

EDITH

I'm sorry; I'm in no mood—

EDIE

For me, Mother, please? I'll sing the man's part.

Physically, a few discreet disparities
Ought to keep us happy as . . .
                    (prompts Edith)
Happy as . . .

EDITH
                    (reluctantly, sourly)
. . . As a clam.

EDIE

Why fight it, lady?
Our star is in ascendance.
Make me your matey—

BOTH

And I'll give you my independence.

(Edie does a soft-shoe. Edith does not. But gradually Edith is buoyed
by her genuine love and affection for Edie.)

GOULD

Come on, Edith, don't tell me you forgot the staging.

EDITH

I didn't forget it, I just don't want to do it.

GOULD

Just do it, and for God's sake, smile.

EDIE

We're a bowl of peaches and cream.

EDITH

The Dodgers and Brooklyn.

EDIE

A permanent team.

EDITH

India and Gandhi.

EDIE

Dagwood and his Blondie.

EDITH and EDIE

Two peas in a pod.

(Edith joins Edie in the dance.)

EDIE

We're an act like Crosby and Hope.

EDITH

A rosy complexion and Ivory soap.

EDIE

Pip and Miss Estella.

EDITH

Hedda and Louella.

EDITH and EDIE

Two peas in a pod.
We stick together
Like a cushion and pins.

EDIE

Birds of a feather.

EDITH

I'd say Siamese twins.

EDITH and EDIE

Ever-aftering where
We will build a cozy retreat
Which no nosy neighbors
Can see from the street.

EDIE

What need we Manhattan?

EDITH

Just us and a cat in—

EDITH and EDIE

A cottage on Cape Cod
For two, please—two peas in a pod.

GOULD

Come on! Dance! A soft-shoe! How can you resist?

EDITH

I can't help myself! It's the music; I'm its hapless victim!

GOULD

Aren't we all, kid, aren't we all?

EDITH and EDIE

If by our devotion
Nature gets the notion
To send a gift from God,
Send two, please.

EDIE

Say kootchie-koo.

EDITH and EDIE

Cuties—

EDITH

In pink and blue.

EDITH and EDIE

Two, please—two peas in a pod.
Two peas in a pod.
Two peas in a pod.

(They embrace on the couch, reunited.)

EDITH

Oh, Edie, it's true. I've been monstrously selfish. Well, have no fear. I'm not going to sing a single, solitary note at your party.

EDIE

Is it because of those awful things that Grandfather said?

EDITH

All eyes should be on you, darling, that's all. You and Mr. Kennedy.

EDIE

Suppose the bride-to-be makes a request?

EDITH

Well . . . if she positively *demands* it . . .

EDIE

Oh, Mother darling, you're an angel. Thank you.

(Edie kisses Edith's cheek.)

Just look at me. I'm still not dressed!

(She flounces up the stairs and pauses on the landing and turns to her mother.)

I love you.

EDITH
(touched but concealing it)
Don't forget! Your grandmother's garters, for luck.

EDIE
I won't!

(Edie bounds upstairs, exuberant. Edith watches after her. Then she returns to the piano, where she pauses at the sight of a family photo. Gould plays the piano quietly underneath.)

EDITH
Do I look like a good mother, Gould? I certainly didn't starve my children. They were very, very nice children. I was absolutely crazy about my two sons. Now Phelan Junior's gone to Texas and Bud's away in school. When Edie's gone, this place is going to seem *enormous.*

GOULD
We have each other, don't we? At least for now.

(Gould stops playing, pours another drink.)

EDITH
What do you mean?

GOULD
You heard the Major. Call me thin-skinned, a sensitive soul . . . *but I don't think the man likes me.*

EDITH
It doesn't matter what he thinks.

GOULD
And with Mr. Kennedy on the horizon . . . Pennsylvania Avenue's a long way from Tin Pan Alley. His kind doesn't look too kindly upon mine.

EDITH
You're *my* friend, and this is *my* house.

GOULD

Your husband's house, Edith. Who knows? Maybe it's time I ate off my own plate.

(beat)

Drank from my own tumbler.

(with significance)

Rumpled my own bedding—

EDITH

Where would you go? How would you live?

GOULD

There's a little place in Hell's Kitchen called The Wrong Man. They'd hire me back. With some new sheet music and a fish bowl—

EDITH

You know you can't go back.

GOULD

Why not?

EDITH

Those old habits of yours—

GOULD

When a poor, lost sailor begs to know the way to the Astor Bar, what am I supposed to do? Ignore him?

EDITH

You've been more faithful to me than the man who promised to be.

GOULD

Oh, Edith. I've tried. But . . .

(He sits back down at the piano, plays.)

(Song: "DRIFT AWAY")

Understand, kid,
It's been just grand, kid.
The cocktails, the cufflinks—the fun.
Remember me when you're singing "Tea for One."

EDITH

If you're gone, who will I even *talk* to?

GOULD

Yourself. The occasional cat.

EDITH

That's not funny.

GOULD

After I'm gone,
When the ocean's haze
Blankets the grounds in grey
Drift away, on the tide,
Drift away.

EDITH

I can't sing a cappella; you know I can't.

GOULD

When you're alone,
And the twilight's glow
Shimmers across the bay
Drift away, on a wave,
Drift away.

EDITH

Darling, please . . . you're my Gibraltar.

GOULD

Our tête-à-têtes—

EDITH

Midnight duets—

GOULD and EDITH

Our breakfast tea and toast.

GOULD

*Funny how things that mean the least
Are what we'll miss the most.*

EDITH

You'll never find a safer haven . . .

GOULD

*Deep in the night
When the whisp'ring breeze
Sings this song I play,
Shed a tear and be glad
For the fun that we had.
Drift away, on a dream . . .
Drift away.*

EDITH

You're my soul mate, that's what you are.

GOULD

"Soul mate." Is that the *nom de jour*?

EDITH

I've no idea what you're talking about.

GOULD

I'll wager you do. And I'm afraid I'm not really living up to my half of
the bargain . . . am I?

EDITH

Please. Don't make it sound so mercenary. You're an artist, Gould. An absolutely *ingenious* artist.

(Gould stops playing. He rises from the piano and says—a bit too pointedly . . .)

GOULD

For the party this afternoon, which would you prefer? Should I wear the white satin jacket you bought for me at Bergdorf's? Or the linen one you picked up in Rome?

(He arches an eyebrow at her for a moment; it seems to pierce her. He touches her cheek, then exits up the stairway.)

EDITH

Now, Gould—! *Gould!*

(Edith stands all alone now—a harbinger of her future, perhaps. She picks up the framed photograph, regards it pensively.)

(Reprise: "THE FIVE-FIFTEEN")

EDITH

Like a photo in a sterling silver frame,
What I wouldn't give
To keep things just the same.
My darling daughter,
Gould and me
Performing songs for company,
Our little family safe . . . serene.

(With apprehension, she looks up at the portrait of her husband, Phelan Beale.)

Will it all be gone at five-fifteen?

(Brooks enters with a telegram on a silver tray.)

BROOKS

Pardon me, but a telegram just arrived, addressed to Miss Beale.

(Edith takes it.)

EDITH

What do you suppose it is?

BROOKS

Heartfelt wishes, I hope.

EDITH

I'll pass them along to her. Thank you, Brooks.

(Brooks exits. Edith tears open the telegram to read it. When she does, her face turns white. She locks eyes with the portrait of Phelan Beale.)

EDITH

Phelan, how could you?

(A door upstairs opens and Joe steps out, spiffy in his tuxedo, humming happily as he descends the stairs to the parlor.)

JOE

Here I am!
                    (executing a "fashion turn")
All set to wait tables or park cars!

(But Edith is still preoccupied, driven to distraction by the contents of the telegram.)

EDITH

Edie's still dressing, is she?

JOE

With a little help from her cousins. I'm afraid it's going to take her twice as long!
                    (girding himself for a little candor)
Look, Mrs. Beale . . . this swell party you've planned . . . Edie appreciates it so much. We both do.

EDITH

(interrupting him)

You love her very much, don't you?

JOE

She's the reason I'm here.

(Edith mixes a drink for Joe, and possibly one for herself.)

EDITH

Some men resent a woman with character. If she's got a staunch constitution, they endeavor to break it.

JOE

Not me; I admire a woman with get-up-and-go.

EDITH

That's terribly modern of you. If only my husband had your generosity of spirit! But no, Phelan's cut from a different cloth.

JOE

Edie says he has a temper.

EDITH

A temper? Ha! When I've lacquered my toenails, or worn my plus-fours to Church . . . Why, the man becomes *unhinged*! Once—steel yourself, Mr. Kennedy—I was asked to sing a *private concert*. To benefit the Ladies Village Improvement Society. "Un Bel Di." Puccini. Well! Phelan was apoplectic. "You will not"—he shouted at me—"You will not sing the role of a common prostitute, Japanese or otherwise!"

(Edith stops herself, abruptly.)

Edie's sure to be happier, isn't she?

JOE

Happier?

EDITH

Promise me you won't forbid her love of the stage.

JOE

A woman should have hobbies. My mother plays bridge.

EDITH

It's more than a mere game with Edie! Why, she's a natural-born performer!

JOE

Oh, we'll have a piano. For sing-alongs, like yours.

EDITH

Sing-alongs?

JOE

With the family. On holidays and such.

EDITH

Edie's told you how she got her nickname, hasn't she?

JOE

Nickname? No, I'm afraid she hasn't.

EDITH

Well, Mr. Kennedy, when I tell you that Little Edie made a splash at the Maidstone Club, I mean it in the most literal way.

JOE

How so?

EDITH

Exquisite diver, our Edie, and there she was . . . poised on the diving board, looking like a veritable swan. And her swimming costume! Beige cloqué; it clung to her like skin on a peach. Well, she went sailing into the water . . . and the seams split. The fabric shriveled up like an accordion, and there she was, in front of all East Hampton, with nothing but her wits!

(Joe blanches a bit.)

EDITH

Well, a lesser girl would've shrieked and run for cover. But not Edie!
No, she swam the length of the pool. *Twice.* And when she climbed out .
. . you know how boys are, Mr. Kennedy, no one offered her a wrap or
even a towel. And Edie had to walk right past them—*all the way to the cabana!*
In that moment her nickname was born—"Body Beautiful Beale."

JOE
(uncomfortable)

Aha.

EDITH

She became the most talked-about girl in town! Why, that's the very
definition of character, isn't it, Mr. Kennedy? To take a scandal and
make it a triumph.

JOE

So she was . . . um . . . popular, was she?

EDITH

I couldn't keep her at home, not anymore! She was off, cruising the
streets in Mr. J. Paul Getty's roadster! Or in Manhattan, at the Twenty-
One Club, enjoying her first sidecar!
(even more confidentially)
You won't find a woman more sophisticated; that's something a man of
your experience is bound to appreciate.

JOE

Look, Mrs. Beale. Edie will be down any minute—

EDITH

Yes. Of course. I'll talk your ear off, if you let me.

(Pause. She reaches out to squeeze his hand.)

I want you both to be supremely happy. That's all.

(Edie's bedroom door opens on the upper landing. She emerges dressed for the party looking resplendent in taffeta and a bold summer scarf. She descends the stairs happily in pointed patent-leather shoes. Joe and Edith watch silently.)

EDIE
(gaily)
I'm not late for my own party, am I?

EDITH
Darling!

JOE
Mrs. Beale. Do you mind?

EDITH
Not at all.
(to Edie)
Sweetheart you look divine.

(Edith exits up the stairs to dress for the party. Edie looks at Joe.)

EDIE
Why the long face, Joe?

JOE
Edie. Your mother—she just told me—

EDIE
I know! She canceled the concert! I've never seen Mother so accommodating. It must be your influence, don't you think?

JOE
It wasn't about music.

EDIE
(concerned now)
Oh no.
(blanching)
She wasn't flirtatious, was she? She has been, you know, with friends of mine. She told Sumner Wadsworth he had a "Renaissance face."

JOE

She's not the one who worries me, Edie.

EDIE

What did she tell you, Joe?

JOE

Body Beautiful Beale?

EDIE
(stricken)

What?
(a beat)

No, she didn't . . . she *wouldn't*. . . .

JOE

It's not about *her,* Edie. It's about *me. My future.*
(then, directly)
Be straight with me. Have there been other fellas?

EDIE

I may have *kissed* once or twice. I may have *held hands*—

JOE

We've done more than kiss, Edie. We've done more than just hold hands—

EDIE

Because you're the one, Joe! Because we said we were *sure*—

JOE

How do I know I'm not "business as usual"—

EDIE

Joe!

JOE

That you'd oblige any fella—any time, any place—*just to get out of Grey Gardens*—

EDIE
(deeply stung)

That's not true!

JOE

But not two minutes ago, your mother sat right here and said—

(Song: "DADDY'S GIRL")

EDIE

Don't believe a word of my mother.
Interfering pain-in-the-can . . .
Burning up with unspoken envy
I got me a bona fide man.

JOE

Don't change the subject—

EDIE

She and Daddy don't have "relations."
Sep'rate rooms with double-locked doors.
"S-e-x" for her and her eunuch
Stopped at the Punic Wars.
I'm my daddy's girl!
Chip off the old man's block.
Yes, my daddy's girl!
Proper and prim as Plymouth Rock.
                    (mimics voice of Phelan)
"Take off that lipstick!"
"Wash off that perfume!"
"How dare you wear high heels!"
As my daddy's girl,
I'm impassioned
By good old-fashioned ideals.

Father will be home soon enough. Talk to him, Joe.

JOE

Why? Because he's willing to cover for you—

EDIE

Because he loves me, Joe, because he isn't *competing . . .*

Mother has a yen for the spotlight.
Daddy disapproves of the stage.
                    (mimics voice of Phelan)
"Never get your name in the papers . . .
Except for the nuptial page."

JOE

Now, Edie—

EDIE

"Modulate your voice to a whisper."
"Always hide your sexual side."

JOE
(shocked)

That's enough!

EDIE

As for "getting drunk" in that frat house—

JOE

What?!

EDIE

—Father O'Hanlon lied.
I'm my daddy's girl!

JOE

What frat house?

EDIE

Virginal as a saint.
That's my daddy's girl!

JOE

Who's Father O'Hanlon?

EDIE

Model of utter self-restraint.
Insinuations! False accusations!
Slander from Harvard boys—

JOE

Who??!!

EDIE

—On a daddy's girl.
I ignore 'em
With charm, decorum, and poise.

JOE

Before he gets married, there are certain things a guy's gotta know—

EDIE

I'm a good girl! A Miss Porter's girl!

All-American apple pie,
Catholic as the Pope's right eye,
In here, Joe—my heart, Joe, I'm pure.
Maybe not like the driven snow . . .
All the same, next to some I know,
Girls who smoke and read Fanny Hill
While I was reading de Tocqueville . . .
Listen to reason.
Let's not be immature.
Honestly, Joe . . .
I thought you said that you were sure.

JOE

I know what I said—

(Edie indicates the portrait of her father.)

EDIE

I'm *his* daughter, Joe, not hers.

JOE

I want to believe you.

EDIE

Then believe me. Believe Daddy. He'll make it right, I know he will—
over a nice Scotch or a Cuban cigar, you'll see—

JOE

Edie, I—

EDIE

Please.

(Joe can't help but relent; he loves her.)

JOE

All right, Edie. *One* whiskey. In his study.

(Edie nods, grateful in every fiber of her body. Joe turns and exits
the room. In Joe's absence, Edie turns to the imposing portrait of
Phelan Beale and speaks to it. The effect is markedly disconcerting.)

EDIE

Tell him I won't just sit in any boy's lap. Tell him that I don't give kisses
for compliments. Some things just aren't worth a fraternity pin. Some
things—
> (a quiet plea)

Tell him only what you know about me, Daddy. *Not what you don't.*

> *I'm my daddy's girl,*
> *Used to his stony glares.*
> *And I know deep down*
> *He's just critical 'cuz . . . he cares.*

EDIE

(imitates father)

"Go find a husband!
Don't waste your life on
Talent you have none of . . . !"
How can any man,
Even Joe,
Match the gift of a father's love?

(Edith descends the stairs, ravishing in her sumptuous summer party dress. A hung-over Gould stumbles down after her, now in his dinner jacket. He collapses at his customary place at the piano.)

EDITH

Steady yourself, babe. You've an hour of cocktail tunes ahead of you.

EDIE

You won't ruin it, Mother. Not this time.

EDITH

What?

EDIE

You won't have the satisfaction—

EDITH

Edie, what are you saying?

EDIE

Your reckless insinuations—your loathsome—your spiteful—

EDITH

She's *executing* me, Gould, but she won't tell me the crime—

EDIE

The *slander*—

EDITH

Slander?!

EDIE

You're jealous, that's all—

EDITH
(caustic now)

Oh yes, that's it! Mama's bitter—

EDIE

Because I've still got my *looks*—my *voice*—my *potential*—

EDITH

Mama's ripe with envy, and you, you're the *cat's meow*—

EDIE

I've a man who loves me, while Daddy would rather spend his nights in
New York City—

EDITH

How dare you?—

EDIE

The moment Daddy arrives—the second he strolls through that door—

EDITH

Oh yes, that doting father of yours—

EDIE

He'll do what he's always done; *he'll clean up the mess you've made of everything*—

EDITH

I won't listen to this!

EDIE

Any man who ever comes close to Grey Gardens, you *frighten* and *bully*
away! I'm telling you, Mother, *you'll die alone!* But not me!

EDITH
(chilly)

Forgive me, darling, but this arrived for you.

(She passes Edie the telegram. Edie stares at it, distrustful. Major Bouvier enters in his dinner jacket as Jackie and Lee trundle downstairs in their matching party dresses.)

MAJOR BOUVIER

Look at my twin virtues! Jackie here looks just like purity . . . and little Lee, Lee must be truth!

(Brooks enters.)

BROOKS
(to Edith)

Train's due any minute, ma'am. Would you like Mr. Beale in his shawl collar, or his peaked lapel?

(Joe enters.)

JOE

Is Mr. Beale here?

(Edith draws herself up.)

EDITH

Aren't you going to open it?

(Silence descends on everyone as Edie opens the mysterious telegram. She reads it aloud.)

(Song: "THE TELEGRAM")

EDIE

"Daughter darling" . . . stop.
"Daddy's little angel" . . . stop.
"All my love and wishes for success
On this joyous"—stop—"thrilling
Permanent, God-willing,
Merge of beauty and noblesse."

MAJOR BOUVIER

Put like a lawyer.

EDIE

"Though regretfully I can't be with you . . ."

ALL

What?!

EDIE

"You must soldier on as if I were."
"My felicities" . . . stop.
"To the Kennedys" . . . stop.
"Tell my wife to demur
From theatrics with that poufter."

GOULD

Stop!

EDIE

"Trust your father.
Learn to honor and obey."

MAJOR BOUVIER

Little late for that.

EDIE

"If the truth be known,
And keep it entre nous,
At present I'm in Mexico with Linda . . . ?"

JOE

Linda who . . . ?

EDIE

"The moment my divorce
From Mrs. Beale is granted,
Come for drinks, we'll be enchanted.
Love from daddy" . . . stop.
"Keeping fingers crossed for you."

(Major Bouvier clears his throat. Edie looks up desolately, heartbroken. Gently, Brooks extracts the telegram from Edie's hand and returns it to the tray.)

BROOKS

So sorry, Miss Beale.

(He exits. Joe shoots Edie a betrayed look.)

JOE

Edie. Looks like that chat with your Dad—

EDIE

Joe. Please—

JOE
(cutting her off)

My parents are due here any minute. If I hurry, perhaps I can still catch them at the Maidstone Club. My father, well . . . I think it's best if I speak to him alone.

EDIE

But you *can't—you mustn't*—

JOE

I wouldn't worry, Edie. Just another scandal you'll no doubt turn into a triumph.

EDITH

You'd better go, Mr. Kennedy.

(Joe goes to her anyway, kisses her forehead quickly. She just sits as stiff as a china doll. He draws himself up and heads out the door.)

JACKIE
(confused)

What is it, Grandpa? What's wrong?

MAJOR BOUVIER

I see two nice, frothy Shirley Temples on the horizon . . . and for
Grandpa, something with considerably more kick.

(He casts a withering look at Edith.)

I wish I had harsh words for your husband, Edith, but I don't. Can't say
I blame him. Not one bit.

(Major turns his attention to his two younger granddaughters, Jackie
and Lee—as Edie watches in disbelief.)

I'm afraid the future of the Bouvier name now rests with you. Make me
proud, ladies. Make me proud.

(Major Bouvier lurches out, the girls on his heels, and shuts
the French doors behind them. Edith and Edie are alone with a
somnambulant Gould.)

EDITH

Linda! A quickie divorce! In *Mexico*! It won't be recognized, not by the
Catholic church.

(Edie doesn't acknowledge her mother. Inside, her mind is racing.)

Pull yourself together, Edie! We've a party. You'll cry, your mascara will
run, and you'll look like an Egyptian. One day, you'll see. Marriage is
for tax codes and Mormons, not freethinkers like ourselves. There's a
lot to be said for living alone. You get to be a real individual. We've got
each other; that's all we need—

(Edie cuts Edith off, a slightly manic look in her eye, her demeanor a
tad off, a bit strident.)

EDIE

I can't stay, Mother. I can't. If I do, I'll vanish. *You'll make me disappear—*

EDITH

What on earth are you talking about?

(Edie starts exploding; words tumble out with unexpected ferocity. Deep within Edie, continental moorings have been set adrift.)

EDIE
(with burgeoning resolve)

I can't go on another year. Another day. Another moment.

EDITH

You're hysterical—

EDIE

I have to get my own place. A hotel room in New York. The Barbizon, maybe—

EDITH

I'll call Dr. Kingsley if I have to—

EDIE

Anyplace but here!—

EDITH

Darling—you're scaring me—

EDIE

Don't! *Don't touch me!*

EDITH

I'm your mother!—

EDIE

I'm not your daughter.
(her hysteria rising)

I'm just your *shadow*, don't you see?

EDITH
(genuinely pained)
Stop this! Please! You're talking *gibberish*—

EDIE
When I get to New York, I'm not *ever* coming back!

(With that, Edie goes up the stairs. Edith turns to Gould, panicked. Then she calls after her daughter.)

EDITH
You don't mean that! Edie! EDIE!

(Edith charges up the stairs after Edie. Brooks enters to find Gould alone.)

BROOKS
The cars are pulling up outside. The guests, they're here.

GOULD
That's Grey Gardens for you. Those on the outside, clamoring to get in, those on the inside, dying to leave. You'd best hold them off; we're not ready.

(Brooks exits. From upstairs, the harsh sound of a door slamming. Edith reappears on the stairs, badly shaken.)

EDITH
She's inconsolable.

GOULD
They're here, Edith. They're gathering on the lawn.

EDITH
What in heaven's name am I going to do?

GOULD
Edith, how I wish I could help you.

(From outside, the sound of milling guests. Edith glances upstairs after Edie a final time. Then she glances toward the garden. She makes a choice. She puts on her best theatrical face. After all, the show must go on.)

EDITH

Brooks, quickly. The doors.

(Brooks swings open the French doors. We hear the sounds of unseen guests. The lights change. Paper lanterns lower. Mustering all her Bouvier pride and dignity, Edith steps out onto the patio, bravely addresses the massing throng of party guests.)

Good afternoon, everyone, and welcome! Welcome to Grey Gardens! I'd like to commence this evening's festivities with a song dedicated to my beloved namesake . . . my darling daughter . . . Miss Edith Bouvier Beale. Gould?

(Stirred, Gould starts to play as Edith sings touchingly with a kind of palpable ache.)

(Song: "WILL YOU?")

When lilacs return in spring,
Will you?
When larks in the meadow sing,
Will you?
When clouds of a summer storm dissolve
And starlight shimmers through,
Will you?
When wild geese of autumn fly,
Will you?
When hearth fires of winter die,
Will you?
Time rushes by.
Memories fade.
Dreams never do.
I will be ever true . . .
Will you?

EDITH

Edie's going to be tickled pink to see you all here. I'm afraid she's slipped away for the moment. The guest of honor! She's missing in action. Nerves, I'm sure.

(Polite laughter from the unseen guests. Meanwhile—inside the house— Edie appears on the landing, traveling valise in hand, a self-styled snood wrapped around her hair.)

But she won't be gone for long! I just know it.

(Edie descends the stairs.)

Just look at the garden! The sound of the ocean! And all of you here, all of you come to celebrate . . . Edie . . . my little Edie . . .

(Edie glances pensively about the living room. She casts a last, lingering look at the portrait of her father. Outside, Edith is oblivious, still hoping, praying . . .)

Why, I've no doubt she . . . any minute now, she'll come breezing down the stairs . . . surprise us, maybe, through the patio doors . . .

(Edie slips out the front door, closing it behind her. She is gone.)

Because I ask you . . .

(Her voice cracks with uncertainty and emotion.)

. . . who could ever bear to leave?

EDITH

When wild geese of autumn fly,
Will you?
As I lay there wond'ring why,
Will you?
Time rushes by.
Memories fade.
Dreams never do.
I will be ever true . . .
Will you?

(The lights change. The walls of the house begin to move, closing in around Edith, framing her in the window, imprisoned. On a scrim, the privet hedges start to climb, crawling up the eaves and over the lintels. The house falls into a deep spell of sleep as . . . the curtain descends.)

ACT TWO

Thirty-two years later, in 1973
Grey Gardens, East Hampton, Long Island, NY

ACT TWO: PROLOGUE—1973

(Underscoring: "GREY GARDENS")

(Through the scrim we make out the house, badly dilapidated and overgrown with out-of-control privet hedges, a neighborhood eyesore. Wind whips through the eaves. We hear the creak of old wood, the rustle of rats, the screech of innumerable cats. The phone rings and rings. No one answers it. We discern the figure of Old Edith, sitting atop the debris of her bed; like one of Beckett's grand dames, plunked down on a mountain of junk. She brays.)

EDITH

WHISKERS! WHISKERS!!

(Another offstage jarring female voice.)

EDIE
(offstage)
MOTHER DARLING, WHAT'S THE MATTER!

EDITH

A CAT GOT OUT! I DON'T KNOW HOW! I THINK HE GOT OUT IN THE HOLE UP THERE . . . !

EDIE
(offstage)
I PUT HIM OUT! YOU TOLD ME TO!

EDITH

NO! HE GOT OUT OF THAT HOLE, EDIE!!

EDIE
(offstage)
"TAKE THE CATS OUT," YOU SAID!

EDITH

DID YOU HEAR WHAT I SAID, WOMAN?

EDIE
(offstage)
I PUT THEM ALL OUT JUST LIKE YOU SAID!

EDITH
LISTEN TO ME, WOMAN! HE GOT OUT THIS HOLE HERE!

EDIE
(offstage)
WHAT??

EDITH
THAT WAS THE NOISE WE HEARD!!

(Again, the phone rings and rings. And still, no one answers it.)

SOME RACCOON DID THAT! MADE A HOLE IN THE WALL!
ISN'T THAT TERRIBLE? THEY'LL HAVE THE WHOLE HOUSE
DOWN SOON!!

EDIE
(offstage)
YEAH, WE'LL BE RAIDED! WE'LL BE RAIDED BY THE VILLAGE
OF EAST HAMPTON! THAT'S THEM ON THE PHONE AGAIN!

EDITH
WHO??

EDIE
(offstage)
THE VILLAGE OF EAST HAMPTON, MOTHER! DON'T ANSWER
IT! LET THEM THINK WE'RE NOT HOME!

EDITH
WHEN ARE WE *EVER* NOT HOME? EDIE? *EDIE!!*

(The scrim rises, fully revealing the ruin of the house and once glorious
gardens, now overgrown by thick brambles.)

SCENE 2—1: YARD

(Enter Little Edie Beale, now fifty-six. Over thirty years have passed since Act One. Edie is played by the same actress who played her mother, Edith, in Act One. Edie is in a highly eccentric ensemble of her own devising. Her face is framed by a black wimple-like snood held in place with an oversized gold brooch clasp. One wisp of grey hair protrudes. She wears heavy, Cleopatra-like eye makeup. Some garments of her outfit are worn "creatively," either upside down or safety-pinned or re-invented from generally unworn articles. She welcomes the audience directly.)

EDIE
Oh, hi! You look absolutely terrific, honestly.
(beat)
Mother wanted me to come out in a kimono, so we had *quite* a fight.

(Song: "THE REVOLUTIONARY COSTUME FOR TODAY")

The best kind of clothes
For a protest pose
Is this ensemble of pantyhose
Pulled over the shorts
Worn under the skirt
That doubles as a cape . . .

(Unfastens her skirt and drapes it on her shoulders as she models Capri pants.)

. . . To reveal you in Capri pants
You fashion out of ski pants
In a jersey knit
Designed to fit
The contour of your shape . . .
Then cinch it with the cord
From the drape.

EDIE

And that's the revolutionary costume for today.
To show the polo riders
In khakis and topsiders
Just what a revolutionary costume has to say.
It can't be ordered from L.L. Bean.
There's more to living than Kelly green.
And that's the revolution I mean.
Da-da-da-da-dum . . .

(Edie holds up a news clipping.)

Just listen to this!

(She reads it aloud using a magnifying glass.)

"*The Hamptons Bee.* July 1972. The elderly, bed-ridden aunt of former
First Lady Jacqueline Kennedy, Mrs. Edith Bouvier Beale—"
                    (glances up at the audience)
My very own mother, can you imagine?—
                    (resumes reading)
"And her adult daughter, Miss Edie Beale, a former debutante once
known as "Body Beautiful Beale"—they called me Body Beautiful Beale.
It's true. That was my . . . whaddayacallit . . . sobriquet—
                    (back to the news clipping.)
"Are living on Long Island in a garbage-ridden, filthy, twenty-
eight-room house with fifty-two cats, fleas, cobwebs, and virtually no
plumbing. After vociferous complaints from neighbors, the Board of
Health took legal action against the reclusive pair."

                    (waving the clipping aloft like a battle flag)

Why, it's the most disgusting, atrocious thing ever to happen in
America!

You fight City Hall
With a Persian shawl
That used to hang on the bedroom wall

EDIE

Pinned under the chin
Adorned with a pin
And pulled into a twist.
Reinvent the objet trouvé.
Make a "poncho" from a duvet.
Then you can be
With Cousin Lee
On Mister Blackwell's list.

(turning a cultured hand into a power fist)

Your full-length velvet glove
Hides the fist.

And that's the revolutionary costume for today.
Subvert the Cris-Craft boaters,
Those Nixon—Agnew voters.
Armies of conformity are headed right your way.
To make a statement you need not be
In Boston harbor upending tea.
And that's a revolution . . . to me.

Staunch!
There's nothin' worse I tell ya'.
Staunch!
S-t-a-u-n-c-h staunch women.
We just don't weaken.
A little-known fact
To the Fascist pack
Who comes here for antique-in.'
Da-da-da-da-dum . . .

Honestly! They can get you in East Hampton for wearing red shoes on a
Thursday and all that sort of thing. I don't know whether you know that.
I mean, do you know that? They can get you for almost anything. It's a
mean, nasty Republican town!

EDIE

The best kind of shoes
To express bold views
Are strapless mules in assertive hues
Like fuchsia or peach,
Except on the beach
In which case you wear flats.
When I stood before the nation
At Jack's inauguration
In a high-heeled pump
I got the jump
On Jackie's pillbox hats . . .

(warns audience)

Just watch it where you step,
With the cats . . .

(Edith screeches from inside the house.)

EDITH

EDIE!!!

EDIE

ALL RIGHT!!

And that's the revolutionary costume pour de jour.
Ya' mix, ya' match, and presto:
A fashion manifesto.
That's why a revolutionary costume's de rigeur . . .

(She glances around the yard through her magnifying glass.)

The rhodendrums are hiding spies.
The pussy willows have beady eyes.
Binoculars in the privet hedge,
They peek at you through the window ledge
With guile . . . !
We're in the revolution,
So win the revolution
With style!
Da-da-da-da-da.

"Oh God. My God. Another winter in a summer town . . ."

Christine Ebersole as Little Edie Beale

"Grey Gardens will be decked out in its prime!"

Sarah Hyland as Jacqueline Bouvier, Christine Ebersole as
Edith Bouvier Beale, Kelsey Fowler as Lee Bouvier, and Bob Stillman
as George Gould Strong

"A musical recital in honor of Miss Edith Bouvier Beale and Mr. Joseph Patrick Kennedy, Jr., the twelfth of July, 1941. Won't Edie be tickled pink?"

Bob Stillman as George Gould Strong and Christine Ebersole as Edith Bouvier Beale

"*I've got the perfect house in mind. Right on Pennsylvania Avenue.*"
Erin Davie as young Little Edie Beale and Matt Cavenaugh
as Joe Kennedy, Jr.

"Edie . . . the last hope of the great Bouvier clan!"

Erin Davie as young Little Edie Beale and John McMartin as
J.V. "Major" Bouvier

"All God's chillun' love hominy grits!"

Kelsey Fowler as Lee Bouvier and Sarah Hyland as Jacqueline Bouvier

"I'm your daughter! Why must you hate me so?"

Christine Ebersole as Edith Bouvier Beale, Erin Davie as young
Little Edie Beale, and John McMartin as J.V. "Major" Bouvier

"Though regretfully I can't be with you . . . "

Bob Stillman as George Gould Strong, Christine Ebersole as Edith Bouvier Beale, Matt Cavenaugh as Joe Kennedy, Jr., John McMartin as J.V. "Major" Bouvier, Kelsey Fowler as Lee Bouvier, Sarah Hyland as Jacqueline Bouvier, Erin Davie as young Little Edie Beale, and Michael Potts as Brooks, Sr.

"The best kind of clothes for a protest pose is this ensemble of pantyhose . . . "
Christine Ebersole as Little Edie Beale

"When are you gonna learn, Edie? You're in this world, you know! You're not out of the world!"

Christine Ebersole as Little Edie Beale and Mary Louise Wilson
as Edie Bouvier Beale

"Yeah, I brought a lot of stuff for your fleas. I'd be more than willing to put it down."

Christine Ebersole as Little Edie Beale and Matt Cavenaugh as Jerry

"But a big gal lights our golden shores!"

Christine Ebersole as Little Edie Beale

"If I ever get out of bed, that—that'll be the 'night at the opera'!"

Matt Cavenaugh as Jerry, Mary Louise Wilson as Edith Bouvier Beale, and Christine Ebersole as Little Edie Beale

"Mother Darling, you don't have enough clothes on."

Christine Ebersole as Little Edie Beale and Mary Louise Wilson as
Edie Bouvier Beale

"The pleasure's all mine. If I don't burn myself."

Matt Cavenaugh as Jerry and Mary Louise Wilson as Edie Bouvier Beale

"A birdcage for a bird who flew away . . . around the world."

Christine Ebersole as Little Edie Beale

EDIE

I have to think these things up, you know.

EDITH

EDIE!!

EDIE

Coming, Mother darling!
> (to audience)

I'm crazy about my mother. She's psychic, and she has a terrific legal brain, and she always tells me what to do. She makes *all* the decisions.
> (a dark laugh)

She has me *absolutely buffaloed*!

EDITH

EDIEEEEE! ARE YOU THERE?

(Edie turns to see Brooks, Jr., the gardener, clipping overgrown privet hedges. He is the son of Brooks, Sr., the butler, played by the same actor.)

EDIE

Oh, Brooks! Is that you, Brooks?

BROOKS, JR.

Yes, ma'am.

EDIE

What a surprise. Everything looks wonderful, *absolutely* wonderful! Your father would have been so proud.

BROOKS, JR.

Thanks, Miss Beale.

EDIE

If think if we're still living next year, I think a vegetable garden would be a good thing in here. Because food's going up. We heard that on the radio last night. It's very expensive to live nowadays. Torturous, really. And Mother and I, we don't have a red cent.

BROOKS, JR.

We're not getting enough sunlight for a garden back here.

EDIE

Mother says she doesn't mind if you have to cut down some privet first.

BROOKS, JR.

All right, then. I'll get right to it.

(Brooks, Jr. exits.)

EDIE
(to the audience, confidentially)

Do you think my costume looked all right for Brooks? I think he was a little amazed!

EDITH

DAMMIT, WOMAN, WHERE ARE YOU? EDIEEEEE!

EDIE
(again, to the audience)

It's very difficult to keep the line between the past and the present. Do you know what I mean? It's awfully difficult.

(She hollers upstairs:)

I SAID I'M COMING, MOTHER!!!

(Edie goes into the house.)

EDITH

Oh, Edie, are you around?

SCENE 2—2: SUN DECK

(Edith, age seventy-nine, sits in a lawn chair on the sun deck. She wears a falling-down bathing suit and her floppy sun hat.)

EDITH

Edie!! The old woman, she has to do everything herself. Edie!!
          (consulting her ledger, writing a check)
Is it the twelfth today? Mr. Brooks Hiers . . . twenty-four bucks, for three cuttings.
          (a beat)
I've got to eat lunch! I'm starving, absolutely starving! I didn't have any breakfast! *Edie!!*

(Edie, in a sunbathing ensemble, slams open the screen door and clomps onto the porch.)

EDIE

I haven't been out of this damn, horrible place in years and years and years. God, if you knew how I felt, I'm ready to kill.

EDITH

Well, they're certainly not going to like *you* at the beach.

EDIE

I suppose I won't get out of here till you die or I die.

EDITH

Oh, that's silly. Oh, Edie, that isn't nice.

EDIE

I never wanted to live in East Hampton, but I was sick and tired of worrying about you, Mother darling! "One night, maybe two," I said to myself. "Until she's herself again . . ."

EDITH

Will you shut up?

EDIE

And then I couldn't leave, I couldn't leave, I couldn't leave—

EDITH

It's a goddamn beautiful day! *Shut up!*

EDIE

I should have stayed put. I had a lovely room at the Barbizon.

EDITH

You got in awful trouble there. I used to send you boxes of groceries!
Big boxes of groceries! You were malnourished! I always thought you'd
have a terrible accident—

(Edie devises a headdress from a sweater.)

EDIE

I should have gotten into nightclub work.

EDITH

Yeah, everything's good that you didn't do.

EDIE

I should have gotten on the stage in Paris at the Follies Bergère!

EDITH

Well, that's the choice! At the time, you didn't want it! You didn't feel
then the way you do now.

EDIE

I always took French, but nothing ever happened there. I can read and
write in French, but I can't speak it. I took years and years and years of
French. Terrible.

EDITH

Everybody thinks and feels differently as the years go by, don't they?

EDIE

"The hallmark of aristocracy is responsibility!" Oh, brother! That *ruined*
me. That *did me in.*

EDITH

Too bad. You missed out!

EDIE

I came down here to take care of my dying mother—

EDITH

I never asked you; I never begged—

EDIE

But then she sprung a fast one on me—she kept right on *breathing*—

EDITH

Edie!

EDIE

She kept right on *walking around*—

EDITH

I'm here, Edie!

EDIE

Talking, too—

EDITH

I'm in the room!

EDIE

Did you hear that? I could've sworn I just heard her voice—

EDITH

Nothing good ever happened to you in New York.

EDIE

Are you kidding? I was discovered by that producer fellow!

EDITH

People discover me every time I leave the house, but I don't think anything of it—

EDIE

Mr. Max Gordon! You've heard of him, haven't you? He discovered Judy Holliday, and he said I was much funnier—

EDITH

Well, you haven't been funny today, boy. You're lacking in humor.

EDIE

He said I was a stitch!

EDITH

It's a good thing you had a place to come home to. To recuperate at Mama's for fifteen, twenty years.

EDIE

But the point is, *I gave it all up*—

EDITH

Everything a person could want, you've got right here.

EDIE

I want freedom.

EDITH

Well, you can't get it, darling, when you're being supported.

EDIE

You can't.

EDITH

You can't get any freedom . . .

EDIE

Yeah . . .

EDITH

. . . When you're being supported.

EDIE

I think you're not free when you're *not* being supported.

EDITH

Nope. Can't.

EDIE

It's awful both ways, I'm thinking.

EDITH

I have no complaints. I have everything I ever wanted.

EDIE

You had a rich husband; you should've stayed with him.

EDITH

I had a perfect marriage . . . beautiful children . . . terribly successful marriage. I never had a fight in my life.

EDIE

Ha!

EDITH

I had a very, very happy, satisfying life.

EDIE

Can't be done. You can't have your cake and eat it, too. Can't.

EDITH

Ohhhh yes, you can. I most certainly did have my cake and eat it, down to the last crumb.

(Song: "THE CAKE I HAD")

EDITH

What good is cake
You have but never eat?
I never could
Deny myself a sweet,
So I sliced my life
And licked the knife
And ate the cake I had.

EDIE

Can't. Can't be done, I'm telling you . . .

EDITH

Two perfect sons
I thoroughly enjoyed.
An absent spouse,
And cats to fill the void,
And the Tri-state's best
Accompanist.
Oh yes, I ate the cake I had.

Moist. Light.
Gaily decorated.
Ev'ry tasty morsel,
Savored, chewed, and masticated.
Young. Bright.
Rich and thin and clever.
Like a second helping?
Sister, would I ever!

EDIE

I'll probably be an old maid until I die. I'll sit around with cats the rest
of my life.

EDITH

When are you gonna learn, Edie? You're *in* this world, you know!
You're not *out* of the world!

The days are gone
When money grew on trees.
The money tree
Came down with elm disease.
But at my age, ducks,
For my two bucks
I'll eat the cake I have
And like it.
I'll eat the cake I have.

EDIE

I think the saddest thing was my not marrying. During the war, my best friend, she was a nurse with the Red Cross . . . She met somebody overseas in a *hospital*. A marine. Lost both his legs at Iwo Jima. Romance was inevitable, really, given the situation.

(a sigh)

But I couldn't travel. Mother wasn't well during the war, you see.

EDITH

Gerald Getty *worshipped* you—and those two nice Rockefeller fellas—

EDIE

They were horrible! Horrible!

EDITH

You just didn't want to get married, and now it's all blamed on me.

EDIE

I missed out on everything.

EDITH

Gripe. Groan.
Point the famous finger.
Life is disappointing,
Put the parent through the wringer.
Sulk. Moan.
Blame it on the mother.
When I'm dead and buried
You won't get another.

EDIE

I met a count in Greenwich Village. He was a poet and a playwright, and he said, "Edith, I want to make an honest woman out of you." I thought that was very decent.

EDITH

He didn't have a nickel in his trousers! Not a nickel!

EDIE

Mother despised him. Gave him the pink slip. To think, I coulda been a countess! Countess Edith!

EDITH

Enough with all
Your celebrated loves.
You had two hands.
You could have modeled gloves.
Is it my fault that
Your cake fell flat?
That you're unmarried,
Bald, and fat?
As the world waltzed by
And Edie sat . . .
I ate the cake I had
And loved it.
Oh, I ate the cake I had,
No thanks to Daddy.
I ate the cake . . . I had.

EDIE

Sometimes I think I have the saddest life . . .

EDITH

You get very independent when you live alone. You get to be a real individual.

EDIE

In New York, I can be a woman. But here I'm just *mother's little girl—*

EDITH

It's very difficult to raise a child fifty-six years of age.

EDIE

I've just got to get to New York City and lead my own life! I don't see *any other future.*

EDITH

You look horrible.

EDIE

My teeth are still all right.

EDITH

You were beautiful when you were young. Your head was exquisite, and you were so gorgeous in hats! It's perfectly foolish of you not to look that way now.

EDIE

I'll have to get another brown tailored suit, and grow my hair.
(laughs, caustic)
My God! I have no hair!

EDITH

You don't want to eat anymore because you've gotten so fat.

EDIE

I can't get my figure back unless I hit New York City. You know . . . that icebox is too near. I can't get away from that icebox!

EDITH

Now I have to sit here and starve all the time. I think I lost five pounds!

(Edie climbs atop a scale. To read the numbers, she peers through binoculars.)

EDIE

How can I eat and catch a man at the *same time*? I'm going to die!

EDITH

Well, don't live with me! I want to eat!

EDIE

I got fat from wearing too many clothes. And sitting down.

EDITH

That's not it *at all*!

EDIE

Just sitting down, you put on weight.

EDITH

It was quarts and quarts of ice cream! Schrafft's French vanilla.
(to audience)
My bill was a hundred and seventy-one dollars, just for ice cream!

EDIE

I ought to take better care of you, Mother darling. Maybe I ought to
give you cooked meals at certain hours. But I don't have any clock.
I never know what time it is.

EDITH

Will you eat some liver pâté?

EDIE

Still, you should eat, you know. Chopped meat and a baked potato
at a certain hour for luncheon. Then a nice little dinner. But that
takes *timing*.

EDITH

I'd just adore a nice liver pâté about now—

EDIE

I have to feed the cats.

EDITH

Later, Edie!

EDIE

But they're famished—positively ravenous—

EDITH

Sure, sure. Feed the cats and starve your mother.

(Edie goes into the house, finds a few cans of what is either cat food . . .
or pâté.)

SCENE 2—3: INSIDE GREY GARDENS

EDIE
(calls to Edith)
They all want luncheon. Did you know that Whiskers disappeared?
I think he got out a hole in the attic. He could jump up there.
(calls out to the cats)
Come on, cats, we're going to have luncheon!
(dumps can into a crusty kitty dish)
Here, kitty. Some nice chopped meat. Doesn't that smell terrific?
No bones in that.

(Gould appears on the staircase landing. Dressed in tones of grey, he
is hidden largely by shadows. Hungrily, hc eyes the dish of cat food that
Edie sets out.)

(Song: "ENTERING GREY GARDENS")

GOULD
When hedges hide the world away . . .

EDITH
Edieee!!!

GOULD
And shadows blur the time of day . . .

EDITH
Edieee!!!

EDIE
I'm feeding the cats!!!

GOULD
When cans of cat food are "pâté" . . .

(Others appear from the shadows.)

ALL
You're entering Grey Gardens.

EDITH

Liver pâté! You have to make it, I can't make it!

EDIE

When am I going to get *out* of here . . . ?

(Edie dumps more cat food into more dishes. Young Edie appears;
followed by all the former inhabitants of Grey Gardens dressed in
shades of grey. They are memories that inhabit the house . . . and
the cats.)

YOUNG EDIE

The musty smell of feline fur.

MAJOR BOUVIER

The dusty marks where pictures were.

JACKIE and LEE

The vermin in the furniture.

ALL

You're entering Grey Gardens.

EDITH

EDIEEE!!!

JOE

The ceiling sags, the stairway creaks.

BROOKS, SR.

The faucet drips, the toilet leaks.

GOULD

The crumbling walls.

MAJOR BOUVIER

The broken clocks.

ALL

It's like a twenty-eight-room litter box.

GOULD

One hundred fifty window sills
To catch a wink or two.

ALL

(yawning)

And that's Grey Gardens
From a cat's-eye view.

EDITH

I'll *die* if I don't *eat!*

BROOKS, SR.

ME-OW!

EDIE

Mother darling! I found your pâté!

MAJOR BOUVIER

ME-OW!

EDIE

I think it's pâté. The label, it's faded . . . is it pâté, or is it giblets for
the cats?

GOULD

ME-OW!

YOUNG EDIE

ME-OW!

ALL

ME-OW!

The fog rolls in, and there it stays.
It suffocates the house in haze.
From room to room, it drifts about
And nobody except a cat gets out.

(Edie clomps upstairs to feed Edith.)

GOULD

A haven from a callous world
With no one sayin' "shoo."

ALL

And that's Grey Gardens
From a cat's-eye view.

EDIE

I may die with this diet. I don't like it at *all*!

YOUNG EDIE

ME-OW!

EDITH

Ever since you started trying to lose weight, you've been impossible.

JACKIE and LEE

ME-OW!

EDIE

I'm not gaining it back.

GOULD

ME-OW!

EDITH

Starve yourself, not me!

BROOKS, SR. and GOULD

ME-OW!

EDIE

Here's your pâté . . . Mother darling!

(Surrounding Edith's bed or laying across it, the others eye the pâté enviously.)

ALL

ME-OW!

(As Edith eats crackers spread with what is either "pâté" or cat food, and the others dine on their luncheon, Edie exits to. . . .)

Scene 2—4: FRONT PORCH

(Edie picks up a tattered old book—it is Zolar's *It's All in the Stars*—and grabs her magnifying glass. Sitting, crossing her legs, she reads aloud.)

EDIE

"The Libra husband is not an easy man to please. The monotony of domesticity is not to his liking, but he is a passionate man and a respecter of tradition."
>(lowers book, struck by a revelation)

All I have to do is find this Libra man!
>(resumes reading)

"The Libra husband is reasonable. He is a born judge, and no other zodiacal type can order his life with so much wisdom."
>(pauses to remark)

My God, that's all I need! Order! That's all I need; an ordered life! You know, a manager! But he's got to be a Libra.

JERRY
>(offstage)

EDIE! HELLO?

(Jerry enters, a teen slacker in a painter's cap and an unruly mop of curls. He wears paint-splattered painter's jeans, T-shirt, and a baseball cap. Jerry is portrayed by the same actor who played Joe Kennedy, Jr.)

EDITH
>(offstage, excitedly)

EDIE! IS THAT JERRY?

EDIE

That's the Marble Faun!
>(to audience)

I call Jerry the Marble Faun. Nathaniel Hawthorne. It's on all the high school reading lists. Terrible, the tragedy connected to the Marble Faun!

EDITH
(offstage)
IS IT JERRY? I HOPE IT'S JERRY!

EDIE
(to audience)
He's Mother's friend, really. I can see it coming. She'll invite him
in . . . let him stay . . . and whaddaya know? He'll be here for years and
years and years. Mother's like that, you know. Doesn't have friends,
really. Just collects strays.

(Jerry steps forward, onto the porch.)

EDIE
Oh, is that you, Jerry? For goodness sake!

JERRY
How ya doin'?

EDIE
Sublime, Jerry, and yourself?

JERRY
Really well.
(beat)
You heard any more from the Board of Health?

EDIE
They keep shoving notices under the screen door. Honestly. They tell
us we have to clean up this mess, and they just contribute to it.

JERRY
I saw your cousin on TV. She gonna help out or what?

EDIE
Oh, I'm terrified of her. She just wants the house, that's all. She got a
lawyer to say I was crazy, and I've always been terribly solid. I asked her,
I said, "If you put me away, where's Mother gonna live? On your yacht
in the Greek islands?" That shut her up. I wouldn't go near any of those
Bouvier people, for God's sake, they're all insane.

(Edie stares at Jerry's feet through binoculars.)

EDIE

What's that around your ankles, Jerry?

JERRY

Hartz Two-in-One.

EDIE

Flea collars? On your feet?

JERRY

So I don't get bit.

EDIE

I almost die with the fleas in this place. I can't go on another year. I have to get to a hotel room.

JERRY

Yeah, I brought a lot of stuff for your fleas.

(Jerry hands her a bag with cans of flea powder. Edie applies some to her legs.)

EDIE

Mother says you're an angel. Our knight in shining armor.

JERRY

I'd be more than willing to put it down.

EDIE

The house is so dirty, isn't it tragic? Mother's room is so filthy; it's just got to be cleaned. And there's that horrible smell. I have pity and fear for anyone who lives downwind of Grey Gardens.

JERRY

Yeah.
                    (beat)
Hey, Edie, you ever find that book?

EDIE

Which book is that?

JERRY

The one I'm named after.
>   (a sheepish grin)
Marble something.

EDIE

Oh, Jerry. Books don't stand a chance, not here. What, with the mold, the pages congeal, and you can't open them.

JERRY

Yeah. Well. If you run across it, I'd kinda like to read it.

EDIE

It's very deep. I'm not sure if you're . . . well. I guess you're up for it.

(Edie raises her magnifying glass again and continues to read from her book on the zodiac.)

EDIE

"The Libra husband does not seek divorce, unless the conditions of his life are not adjustable."
>   (looks up from book, shakes her head)
Jerry, darling, you're Aquarius, aren't you?

JERRY

Yeah.

EDIE

>   (sighing dejectedly)
New York City's the only place for me. I simply gotta get up a little nerve. Do you think I oughta get into show business? That sorta thing?

JERRY

I dunno, Edie. Can you sing or dance?

EDIE

Are you absolutely crazy? There isn't anything I can't do! What, you think I'm gonna look funny dancing? I do terrific dances! Wait here.

JERRY

But, Edie, I gotta—

EDIE

WAIT.

(Edie exits into the house.)

I danced eight hours last night, practicing this marching song! My God, my muscles! They're gone, with this soft life!

(Jerry sits on the stoop, pulling off his shoe. Idly, he plucks at his toenails. Inside, Edie continues to shout out to him.)

This is the march they played at Joe's funeral. Joseph Patrick Kennedy! Nineteen Forty-Four! He was on a top-secret mission; the bombs exploded while he was still inside the plane. All the boys I danced with, they died in World War II. You know, the great heroes, from the best families. I suppose they were the bravest.

JERRY

Yeah, sure.

EDIE

They always sent the best to fight; they should've sent the sick ones! Then the whole thing would've been over. You know, the ones that had physical things wrong. Then the wars wouldn't have lasted. They just couldn't have done it with people that weren't always feeling absolutely wonderful.

JERRY

Maybe you should write a letter. President Nixon.

(Edie bursts through the screen door onto the front porch of the house, a vision in a fire-engine red snood, red knit sweater, red tights, red pinned skirt, and white flats.)

EDIE

They should outlaw war, don't you think? War should be against the law.

JERRY

You're dressed for battle, Edie.

(Edie hunches forward, reaches inside her outfit to adjust her slipping breasts.)

EDIE

I only hope my costume stays up . . .

(She dashes back in to put her music on the hi-fi. From inside, we hear a scratchy old WWII recording of a home front "victory" march. Then Edie reemerges, waving a little American flag.)

(Song: "THE HOUSE WE LIVE IN")

EDIE

La-da-da-da-da-dum!
Ta-da-da-da-da-dum!
Da-da-da-da!
Da-da-da-da!
Da-da-da-da—whoops!

(glancing down at her costume)

My God, do you think it's going to stay up?

(coyly adjusting her chest)

I feel something slipping . . . I feel something . . .

(Pointing the little flag flirtatiously at Jerry, she performs to the record. Jerry watches, occasionally reaching down to pick his toes.)

EDIE

It's a big house,
The house we live in!
Big hit, this.
It's a big job
Guarding freedom's doors!
World War Two . . .
It's a big foe
Across the ocean . . .
That means Hitler . . .
But a big gal
Lights our golden shores!

                       (waves little flag)

And wheee!
With a big heart
Here on the home front
. . . just exhausting!
Every little guy pitch in!
Here comes the good part . . . !
March! March!
March to buy your war bonds
So the house we live in will win!

(Summoned by Edie's mind, the singers of the old record appear costumed in navy blues.)

La–da–da–da–da–dum!
Ta–da–da–da–da–dum!
Ten–hut!
Company—fall in!

RECORD SINGERS

It's a big house,
The house we live in!

EDIE

My *God!*

RECORD SINGERS

It's a big job
Guarding freedom's doors!

EDIE

Windows and doors!

RECORD SINGERS

It's a big foe
Across the ocean . . .

EDIE

Anchors aweigh!

RECORD SINGERS

But a big gal
Lights our golden shores!

EDIE

Big as Staten Island!

RECORD SINGERS

Till the big day
We storm the beach front—

EDIE

That means D-Day.

RECORD SINGERS

And we liberate Berlin—

EDIE
(explains to Jerry)

You weren't born yet.

EDIE and RECORD SINGERS

—March! March!
March to buy your war bonds
So the house we live in will win!

JERRY

Cool.

RECORD SINGERS

Be alert.

Stand your ground.

Check the sky
If a siren should sound.

Pull your weight.

Do your share.

Keep recruits
On their chutes in the air.

Over land, over sea,
Fight to keep the free world free. . . .

EDIE

Dip and glide.

Stand aside.

My pulse is pounding!

Work those thighs.

Slenderize.

Where did all my hair go?

I need an agent!

EDIE and RECORD SINGERS

As we march! March!
Marching for each other!
Every man-Jack,
Junior miss and mother
'Cause we all are
One another's brother,
One big family under the skin!
And the house we live in will win!

(As the record ends, the record singers vanish. The lights return to as before. Edie is alone on the porch with Jerry. There is the sound of a plane overhead. Edie stops twirling, momentarily rattled by the plane. She looks up at the sky, disoriented.)

EDIE

See? When they do that, that's when the planes flew over. A tribute, before they buried him. I've got to get it all coordinated *in my mind—*

(Edith shouts from upstairs.)

EDITH

EDIEEE! Is that him? IS THAT JERRY?

EDIE

I'm working on my DA-ANCE!!!

(Picking his toes, Jerry watches Edie twirl rapturously around in a circle.)

Darling Jerry, where have you been all my life? Where have you been, where have you been, where have you been, where have you been? The only thing I needed was an audience!

EDITH

JERRY! EDIE! HELLO?

EDIE

An audience! That's all I needed!

EDITH

IS ANYBODY THERE?

EDIE

Goddamn it, Mother—

EDITH

LET JERRY IN! HURRY UP!

(Edie stops dancing. Her body goes limp; a study in defeat.)

EDIE

Mother is screaming for you to go up. You want to go up?

JERRY

Sure.

(They enter the house, Jerry first. Edie follows him through the screen door, singing to herself, waving her little flag.)

EDIE

It's a big house,
The house we live in . . .
It's a big job
Guarding freedom's doors . . .

SCENE 2—5: EDITH'S BEDROOM

(Edith is half naked in her garbage-strewn bed, poking at a pot of corn simmering on an electric hot plate.)

EDITH

SHE'S TRYING TO MURDER ME, JERRY! I WAS FROZEN THIS MORNING WHEN I WOKE UP! SHE ONLY LEFT ME ONE LITTLE KITTY TO KEEP WARM—AND ALL THESE BLANKETS WERE ON THE FLOOR—

(Edie and Jerry enter.)

Jerry! You're puffing and blowing. Was it the stairs? Oh God, the other day I almost tripped! I almost broke my neck! Edie, you've simply *got* to pick up a mop!

EDIE

Not today, Geraldine.

EDITH

Stairs wear you out, Jerry?

JERRY

No, I'm tired. I don't want to get any tireder.

(Edie points at Jerry surreptitiously and whispers to Edith.)

EDIE

Mother darling, you don't have enough clothes on.

EDITH

I'm gonna get naked in just a minute, so you'd better watch out.

EDIE

That's what I'm afraid of.

EDITH

Yeah, for what? Why? I haven't got any warts on me!

EDIE

That isn't the point, Mother darling.

EDITH

Have I, Jerry? I haven't got any warts on me!

JERRY

You look like a night at the opera, Mrs. Beale.

EDITH
(delighted)

Oh, that's too much. Jerry, you're too much. If I ever get out of bed, that—that'll be the "night at the opera"!

(As Edith stirs the pot of corn, Edie brings a stick of margarine from the small fridge.)

See, Jerry? I gotta do everything myself. She's no cook, and she's no waitress! What do you want, dear? You want a nice piece of corn?

JERRY

No, I don't want any, thanks.

EDITH

You're not going to drink anything?

JERRY

No.

EDITH

You mean to say you're not going to have a drink or a highball or something like that? Don't you think you better have some rum?

(Jerry pokes around in the small fridge.)

Jerry, I'm badly treated all along. Where's your plate?

(Jerry passes her a plate.)

JERRY

Oh hell. I can't resist. I'm starving.

EDITH

Which piece of corn do you want, Jerry?

JERRY

Doesn't matter.

EDITH
(to Edie, favorably impressed)
See how polite he is? You want something, Edie?

(Edie seats herself on the other twin bed.)

EDIE

No.

EDITH

You sure?

EDIE

I don't *want* any!

EDITH

Jerry, you want to put some margarine on, don't you?

JERRY

Yeah. You wanna do it for me?

EDITH

Why, yeah. The pleasure's all mine. If I don't burn myself.

(Edith rubs a stick of margarine, still in its wrapper, on Jerry's corn as
he holds it.)

JERRY

Ow! 'S hot.

EDITII

You have a beautiful face, Jerry, like a girl.

JERRY

I got very big hands.

EDITH

Like . . . you look like my mother. The absolute image of my mother, Jerry.

(Jerry bites into the corn. He savors it. We hear the crunch of his bite, the smacking as he chews noisily, the slurping sounds as he licks his fingers clean. Edith listens, in rapture.)

(Song: "JERRY LIKES MY CORN")

EDITH

Jerry likes the way I do my corn.
Isn't he a treasure?
More corn?
Lookit how he chows right through my corn.
It's my only pleasure.
I boil it on the hot plate
Till all the juice is gone.
Bless his soul,
He knows which side
My corn is buttered on.

(Jerry grunts in appreciation.)

Jerry lacks a mother's tender care.
Nobody to need him.
Mothers now are barely ever there.
Someone's gotta feed him.
The kind of things that I like
His high school friends all scorn.
Cottage cheese. Chamomile.
Dr. Norman Vincent Peale.
But Jerry likes . . . my corn.

EDITH
The things you do for me! Jerry, you're my Gibraltar!

EDIE
(drily)
You're a regular Major Domo, Jerry.

JERRY
The corn's out of this world.

EDITH
(flattered)
Oh, did I do it nicely? He always compliments me on the way I do my corn.

JERRY
I was thinking . . . if you wanted . . . I could get some germicide. I was thinking, maybe, a tarp.

EDITH
Why, Jerry, you're extravagant. You spoil us. Doesn't he just spoil us, Edie?

EDIE
Oh, sure.

JERRY
Hey, before I forget. The old McAllister place, over by Georgica Pond? I was ripping out their kitchen. They got a washing machine, getting a new one, real nice, a Whirlpool in avocado. Thing is, *they said I could keep the old one.* I was thinking I could bring it over here, hook it up. That way, you could wash your clothes once in a while. Maybe even your bedding. No offense, Mrs. Beale, but I saw some, uh, insects in your sheets. "Red coats," I think. That can't be good for ya'. A washing machine'd clean that right up. Whaddaya think?

EDITH

Jerry is a son like my own two.

EDIE

Sons who never phone you.

EDITH
(to Jerry)

Salt?

(to Edie)

Boys have more important things to do.

EDIE

After they disown you.

(Jerry grunts.)

EDITH

And though he hardly says much,
I understand his grunts.
"Hey" means "hi."
"Yo" means "yes."
Believe me, he's no dunce.

(Edie raises her eyebrows.)

EDITH

Anything that breaks, he knows which tool.
Jerry is a fixer.
Not *her.*
Happy hour starts right after school.

(She hands Jerry an alcoholic drink in a jelly jar glass. She herself is not allowed any.)

Jerry, have a mixer.

(Jerry grunts.)

EDITH

He tells me things the kids like,
And I just feel reborn.
Mountain Dew. Super Bowl.
Sex 'n' drugs 'n' rock 'n' roll.
But most of all . . . my corn.

Jerry, you know what I'd like? Some music. I'm happier when I'm singing than anything I've ever done since I was born. See if you can find . . . that song. The one I just adore—

EDIE

Oh sure. "The Girl Who Has Everything."

EDITH

No, heaven's no . . . the flipside. Jerry knows. We've sung it before, haven't we, Jerry? Jerry knows the one.

JERRY

Yeah. I think I saw it downstairs.

EDITH

I have to get my voice exactly back the way it was when I was forty-five years old.

EDIE

Let me help, Mother darling. I'm extremely organized. I know exactly where to look for that record.

EDITH

No, let Jerry.

EDIE

I've got it under control, kid. I can find it.

EDITH

Jerry can find things in this house—right on this bed—you couldn't find for half an hour.

(She smiles at Jerry. He nods, grins at Edie—victorious—then exits.)

EDIE

I'm so sick of that kid! I mean, I have great pity for him, and I like
him, but . . .

EDITH

My soul mate. That's what he is. That's the word.

EDIE

He steals things! From my room!

EDITH

Oh, he does not.

EDIE

Books mostly! He takes them from my room, and he hides them in the
attic! He already took the glassware, and pretty soon, the antiques will
be gone!
> (confidential whisper)

I'm telling you, Mother, you shouldn't have contact with the outside
world. If you get what I mean . . . you can't tell what's been put *in,* or
what's been taken *out.*

EDITH
> (to audience)

The trouble is, she's madly in love with him.
> (pleased at her mischief)

Pardon me, but it's true!

EDIE

Well, he might as well leave right now 'cause he's *never* gonna get it.
So *that's* it.

EDITH

Get what? Sex—with *you?*

EDIE

Well, that's all they're after. That's all they're after.

EDITH

An old person like you? Good God!

EDIE

So you might as well tell him right now to forget about it . . .

EDITH

Jerry doesn't want any sex with you!
Jerry likes his own age!

EDIE

Ohhhh yes.

EDITH

Kids of seventeen do not pursue
Relics of the Stone Age!

EDIE

Believe me, *I* can tell these things . . .

EDITH

Jerry doesn't want any sex with you!
Jerry isn't crazy!
Adolescent girls now are easy lays . . .
                    (to audience)
Same as Edie in her "awkward phase."
                    (obliquely, to Edie)
Jerry's got a new girl ev'ry night . . .
And not a one of 'em have cellulite.

EDIE

He's gonna be here and for *years and years*! It's gonna be one of those things like . . . George Gould Strong all over again! The two of you, conspiring like you do. And me! What about *me*?!

EDITH

Who said anything about you? I didn't hear it . . .

EDIE

People I used to know at the Maidstone Club for years and years! Now they see me and they cross the street—

(Suddenly, there is an odd banging noise from the attic. Edie stops, looks up, listens.)

EDIE

Uhhh . . . there he is. Upstairs. Hear him?

EDITH
(humoring her)
Oh sure. Yeah, he's up there. I hear him.

EDIE

I swear, everything is up in that attic . . .

EDITH

That's not Jerry!

EDIE

Of course it's Jerry!

EDITH

IT'S YOUR RACCOON, EDIE!—Jerry is *my* company! He likes my corn, in my bedroom!

EDIE

He's going to be here for years and years.

EDITH

He doesn't want any sex with *you*! Get out of here!

EDIE

I want the people I want in this house—

EDITH

Go away! You're making me very angry! Go out and . . . go out and . . . *go out and run to your raccoon!*

(Rejected, Edie stomps out of the room. Alone now, Edith reflects to herself.)

EDITH

Jerry doesn't fight like two fishwives.
Jerry likes relaxing.
Me too.
Now and then we play my forty-fives . . .
Hear the old sad sack sing.
No picnic growing older,
Abandoned and forlorn . . .
Stuck in bed, stiff with gout.
Alcoholic drinks are out.
"You'll die,"
The doctors warn . . .
Then quick as a wink,
I'm in the pink
'Cuz Jerry likes . . . my corn.

I tell you, that boy is a *gift*.

SCENE 2—6: THE ATTIC

(Alone in her retreat in the attic, Edie is surrounded by mementos, shells, trinkets, boxes, her old bedroom mirror, and the portrait of Mr. Beale that once hung proudly in the parlor, now streaked with age.)

EDIE
(with an edge of panic)

Guess what happened! What I felt was in the cards. *The Marble Faun is moving in!* He just gave us a little washing machine. That cements the deal! I can't bear it, I'm telling you . . . !

(Song: "AROUND THE WORLD")

It's my mother's house
In my mother's name,
And you can't beat Mother
At Mother's game.
'Cuz she likes the people
Who I don't like,
And if I don't like it
It's "take a hike,"
Which is Mother's way
Of reminding me
When you live off Mother
You can't be free,
So I think that Mother
Is very mean . . .
And this latest thing?
With this wash machine?
The one Jerry brought.
Don't be too surprised
If the guy moves in,
And I'm pulverized
'Cuz I'm damned if I'm
Gonna waste my time
Washing clothes in that goddamn machine!!

(In an abrupt change of temperament, she turns to her collection of artifacts: an old "Around the World" poster, a silver mask from a costume party, shells from the beach.)

EDIE

I feel so strongly about mementos. Memorabilia, I guess you'd call it . . .

(She arranges them artfully on the wall of the attic, tacking them up with thumbtacks and standing back to admire.)

> *"Around the World"*
> *Is what I call*
> *My wall of special things.*
> *Around the world*
> *With rose bouquets*
> *I dried and tied on strings.*
> *A silver mask from a masquerade.*
> *Around and 'round I twirled . . .*
> *You tack them up*
> *So you can twirl around the world . . .*

(From downstairs, Edith calls.)

EDITH

EDIE!! HE FOUND IT! JERRY FOUND MY OLD SONG!

EDIE

(angry again)

> *It's my mother's house*
> *And my mother's friends,*
> *And with Jerry coming, it never ends.*
> *It's the same old story*
> *As George Gould Strong.*
> *Not in twenty years did we get along!*
> *Though I do feel bad*
> *For the way he died,*
> *In a two-bit flea-bag, a suicide . . .*

EDIE

It was Mother's money,
The Bouviers'
And if mother spends it
In crazy ways
No one else "took care" of her,
Only me!
She was taken care of—
Not "sex-u-ally"!
And if you infer
They were using her,
I will shove you right under the goddamned bed!!

Around the world
With stones and shells.
The nicest one I lost.
Around the world
Without a boat
On just a quote from Frost.
"Two roads diverged in a yellow wood . . ."
And I explore them all,
Around the world.
The world around the attic wall . . .

Around the world
There isn't room
For every special thing.
Around the world
You choose a few
To make the music sing.
A silver mask from a masquerade,
Around and 'round I twirled . . .
You tack them up
So when you go
The world will be
The one you know . . .

(She holds up an old birdcage.)

EDIE

A birdcage I plan to hang.
I'll get to that someday . . .
A birdcage for a bird
Who flew away . . .
Around the world.

(Following the song, silence. Then—in the midst of the quietude—we hear a tinny recording of an old song coming from Edith's bedroom. It is a record of Edith singing "Will You?" accompanied on the piano by Gould —the same song she sang in the first act at Edie's engagement party when Edie left home. Up in the attic, Edie listens, mesmerized. The scene shifts to . . .)

SCENE 2—7: EDITH'S BEDROOM

(Edith sits in bed as the platter spins. Jerry lounges nearby, listening.)

(Underscoring: "WILL YOU?")

EDITH
I cut this record in 1938 with my accompanist, Mr. George Gould Strong. He was the most brilliant man I've ever met, that's including Mr. Beale and Mr. Bouvier! Completely brilliant—

JERRY
Sorry, Mrs. Beale, I got to be going.

EDITH
(too smitten by the music to pay Jerry any mind)
He was a writer. He wrote seven books at one time, and he played the piano magnificently, and composed exquisite music, and dedicated about eighty songs to me.

JERRY
I'll stop by tomorrow, with some brick jointers. We'll get the place fixed up, best we can, before the inspection.

EDITH
I was very serious about my singing. Loved it. Then I met Mr. Beale, and the jig was up.

JERRY
Tell Edie so long, okay?

EDITH
After that, I did all my singing right here. In the house. In the parlor downstairs. Wasn't the same, really.

JERRY
I'm going to your purse now, and I'm taking out five dollars. Watch me now. I'm only taking a fiver; I'm putting the rest back. Okay?

EDITH
(sighs wistfully)
The tune is wonderful! Isn't that the most beautiful . . . ?

JERRY
You be good now, Mrs. Beale. You take care of yourself.

(Jerry slips out unnoticed by Edith.)

EDITH
The last time I performed this song . . . When was it, I can't remember
. . . summertime, I think. The garden was in bloom; the lawn, it
was *teeming* with people . . . I was in fine voice, I know that, each note
a clarion . . . pure as Venetian glass! "Brava, brava! Encore!" The
occasion . . . what was it . . . the old woman, she can't recall . . .

(Edith warbles along with the recording of her younger self. Edie
enters quietly.)

Will youuuu . . . ?

EDIE
(appreciatively)
No one could compete against Mrs. Beale and Gould.

EDITH
(echoing the record again)
Will youuu . . . ?

EDIE
No one in the world. Imagine bothering about anything when you had
a talent like that!

EDITH

. . . Dreams never do!
I will be ever true . . .
Will youuu . . . ?

(Swept away for a moment, Edie starts to sing along with the recording, too.)

                                    EDIE
Will youuuu . . . ?

(Edith stops singing. She looks at EDIE, disapproving.)

                                   EDITH
You're singing it incorrectly. Very ugly. Always must do everything correctly.

                                    EDIE
Hmm–hmm–hmm–hmmm . . .
Will youuuu . . . ?

                                   EDITH
Don't say "youuuuu" like that! You're not Czechoslovakian.

(Edie continues singing and swaying as Edith grows increasingly disconcerted.)

                                   EDITH
                               (to audience)
You see, she knows she sings so badly that she has to wiggle about twenty times to every note. To distract you people, because she really can't sing it right.

                                    EDIE
Will youuu . . . ?

                                   EDITH
That's not it! You're *waaaaaay* off the beat there! Go to the bottom of the class!

(The more Edie is chastised by her mother, the more she starts to deliberately massacre the song. Her voice turns loud and shrill.)

EDITH

Don't make funny faces! Everything is perfectly disgusting on account of you! Would you bring me my little radio? Please? I have got to have some professional music!!

(Wreaking more havoc, Edie begins to dance.)

Oh, Edie, I can't take it! I'm your mother, remember me? Stop it, will you? I want my radio! STOP IT!!

(Edie deliberately yanks the needle across the record, scratching it. The music abruptly stops.)

EDIE

I stood for you all these years.

EDITH

Well, of course you did! You'd no place else to go—

EDIE

Not true, kid! I was going to the White House!

EDITH

Oh, Edie!

EDIE

I was! With Mr. Joseph Patrick Kennedy.

EDITH

Pick up a fresh paper; that's yesterday's news!

EDIE

He was simply *keen* for me, but you got rid of him because he came from a *celebrated family*—

EDITH

I did no such thing!

EDIE
(to audience)
Mother didn't want me to have anybody that was *decent,* you understand—

EDITH
That's the way! Pin it all on Mama!

EDIE
You got rid of him in *fifteen minutes flat*—

EDITH
You didn't need me for that!

EDIE
Fifteen minutes, that's all it took—

EDITH
You did that all by yourself—

EDIE
And poor Joe Kennedy was out the door!

EDITH
You scared him off but good, sister!

EDIE
(to audience)
She's very mean to me!

EDITH
Oh, she's just acting all over the place—

EDIE
I think you were very cruel—

EDITH
Edie, really! This is too much—

EDIE

I think Mother was absolutely cruel! To drive my only beau away!

EDITH

I didn't want my child to be taken from me! I'd be entirely alone!

EDIE

I never had a minute's fun! Not a minute—

EDITH

You had your chance; all those years in New York—

EDIE

You pressured me to come home, so I did—I got on the train—
I came back—

EDITH

That's not what happened—

EDIE

You made me leave the BARBIZON!

EDITH

You'd been there long enough—

EDIE

But I was getting my big chance!

EDITH

You were getting lines in your face—

EDIE

I was getting my big audition! In 1952!

EDITH

Oh, you were not!

EDIE

I was going to get it!

EDITH

Well, you didn't—

EDIE

You made me come home!

EDITH

Damn it, woman—I'll have to start drinking!

EDIE

And I was sick and tired of worrying about you, day and night—

EDITH

You'll make a drunkard out of your mother!

EDIE

I felt a deep responsibility for you, kid—

EDITH

You didn't have to worry the way you did. I had a very good man—a very good man to take care of me—

EDIE

Nobody took care of you! I took care of you!

EDITH

I never had any words with Mr. Beale at all.

EDIE

And I took care of this damn house, for twenty-five years!

EDITH

After Mr. Beale got his Mexican divorce, I wanted him to come home! I wrote him a letter on engraved stationery, and I told him all was forgiven and he was to come back here—back to Grey Gardens—

EDIE

As long as my father was alive—*my father was alive*—

EDITH

So we could be a family again, like other families—

EDIE

He wanted to run my life!

EDITH

But Edie said no—

EDIE

I was scared to death of him—

EDITH

She said she'd leave the house forever—

EDIE

I didn't want him here—

EDITH

Just imagine!

EDIE

Screaming at me all the time—

EDITH

She said she'd *up and leave*—

EDIE

"Take off that lipstick!"—

EDITH

If Mr. Beale ever came back to Grey Gardens!—

EDIE

"Wash off that perfume!"—

EDITH

She actually threatened to run away—

EDIE

"How dare you wear high heels!"—

EDITH

If *my husband—her father*—came back!

EDIE

I didn't need the aggravation—the *humiliation*—!

EDITH

Tell the truth, Edie—

EDIE

I knew if Mr. Beale came back, I'd *never* get married!

EDITH

That's not the reason!

EDIE

I'd *never* find a man!

EDITH

That's not it at all!

EDIE

Mother! Please!

EDITH
(angrily warning)

Edie . . . !

EDIE
(furiously trumping her)

He'd have had me committed!!!

(A momentary silence. The mood shifts.)

EDITH
(delicately now)

You needed to come home.

(Edie turns steely and silent. Too much has been said. Like an automaton, she plucks the transistor radio from the bureau and marches to her mother's bed. Her voice is strained and arch.)

EDIE

Your radio, Mother darling.

(Edie turns on the radio, drops it in Edith's lap, and exits, leaving Edith in semi-darkness, alone. Edith picks up the transistor radio. A burst of static—and it comes to life.)

ANNOUNCER ON RADIO

From the world-famous Marble Collegiate Church, it's time for *The Positive Prayer Hour* with Dr. Norman Vincent Peale!

(Dr. Norman Vincent Peale, played by Major Bouvier, appears dimly, as if right in the bedroom with his choir. The robed choir singers are the others. The organist is Gould. Edith clutches the radio to her bosom for company, rocking ever so gently to the music, hoping in vain for comfort from it.)

(Song: "CHOOSE TO BE HAPPY")

N. V. PEALE

Harsh winters weather
The mansions we build.
Highways have potholes,
And milk will be spilled.
Does your cup runneth
Half empty or filled?
One simple principle
Makes you invincible:

Choose to be happy!

CHOIR

Happy! Happy!

N. V. PEALE

Choose to be happy!

CHOIR

Happy! Happy!

N. V. PEALE

Make that the motto
You use to be happy.
Happy to choose what
You choose not to see.
Everybody!

N. V. PEALE and ALL

Choose to be happy like me!

EDITH
(nodding her head, repeats to herself)
. . . like me.

(Simultaneously, up in her private retreat in the attic, Edie is taking action. She drags out a suitcase and begins to pack her mementos.)

N. V. PEALE

Think, really think
Of a goal worth achieving,
Then try, really try,
But begin by believing.
Wake every morning
And say, really say:
The rest of your life starts today!

CHOIR

Hallelujah!
Hallelujah!
Hallelujah!

N. V. PEALE
(to Edie)

You're on your way . . . !

(N. V. Peale indicates for a young woman in the choir to step forward and "testify.")

Sister Marla . . . ?

(Sister Marla—played by Young Edie—steps forward as Edie packs. A train whistles in the distance.)

SISTER MARLA (YOUNG EDIE)

Sandcastles crumble
As evening rolls in.
Look to the sunrise
About to begin.

(Young Edie lays a scarf across the attic railing, the same scarf she wore when she left home the first time.)

You're goin' places
You never have been.

N. V. PEALE and SISTER MARLA

Get up the nerve to be
All you deserve to be!

CHOIR

Choose to be happy!
Happy! Happy!
Choose to be happy!
Happy! Happy!
Make that the motto
You use to be happy.

N.V. PEALE

Positive thinking!

Make up your mind!

Happy to choose what
You choose not to see.

N. V. PEALE

You'll see how happy you'll be!
If you will . . .

(As tears roll down Edith's cheeks, Edie shuts her suitcase, buttons her old fur coat, and heads downstairs to the front door with a resolve we haven't seen before, choosing to be happy . . . by leaving home.)

ALL

. . . Choose to be happy!
Happy! Happy . . . !
Choose to be happy!
Happy! Happy . . . !
Choose to be happy!
Happy! Happy . . . !
Choose to be happy!
Happy! Happy . . . !

(As the radio dies down, Edie clomps down the stairs and out the front door to . . .)

SCENE 2—8: THE FRONT YARD

(. . . But on reaching the front yard, Edie abruptly stops. The cool evening air carries a chill. The garden is barren of greenery in the dusk of late autumn. Something in Edie's resolve begins to crack ever so slightly. Looking at the empty branches in the wind, she sings in a halting, tentative voice.)

(Reprise: "AROUND THE WORLD")

EDIE

Around the world
Beyond the wall
Before the haze rolls in
Above the trees
Into the clear
Up where the clouds grow thin . . .

(She takes a few reticent steps forward, down the walk toward the garden gate.)

Across a sea glistening with gold
I'll take the wind and soar.
You're almost there.
You're out the door.
It's not too late.
A few steps more.
Around the world,
New worlds await.
Just flip the latch,
And through the gate . . .
Go through the gate . . .
The garden gate . . .
My mother's gate . . .

(She stands, frozen. Try as she might, she cannot bring herself to flip the gate latch. In the twilight, a figure passes the house. It is Brooks, Jr.)

BROOKS, JR.

Privet's all cut, ma'am. I'm done for the day.

(a beat)

Miss Beale? You all right?

(Edie nods, self-conscious.)

You going out? Well, that's something. That's new. You're smart to bundle up. It's going to drop tonight. You can already feel the chill.

(He stares at her a moment. Edie seems "off." He construes that something is awry.)

Ma'am . . . ? You need some help? You want me to walk you to the station, or call you a cab?

EDIE

No, thank you. I've got it under control here. I'm extremely organized.

BROOKS, JR.

All right, then. Just asking. G'night.

(Brooks continues on his way. Church bells toll in the distance. Alone, Edie stares morosely at the barren branches, listens to the wind in the trees, pulls her fur coat tightly around her.)

(Song: "ANOTHER WINTER IN A SUMMER TOWN")

EDIE

Another winter.
The renters go home.
The maple goes from crimson to brown.
Oh God . . .
My God . . .
Another winter in a summer town.

EDIE

The beach is empty.
They cover the pools.
The patio umbrellas come down.
Oh God . . .
My God . . .
Another winter in a summer town.

One little leaf
Adrift in the breeze
Refuses to fall from the sky.
Blown by the wind
It clings to the trees,
Unwilling to wither and die. . . .

The summer's over,
But I'm still a girl
Cavorting in my carnival crown.
From blossom to blossom,
I buzz like a bee.
Then glance in the mirror,
And who do I see?
A middle-aged woman
Inhabiting me
Because it's winter in a summer town.

Ah-ah-ah-ah-ah-ah . . .

(As Edie remains in the yard, the lights rise upstairs on Edith in her bed, contemplating winter, the end of her days, crooning vaguely remembered fragments of an old, sad song, probably one written for her by Gould.)

EDITH

Ah-ah-ah-ah-ah . . .

(Lights reveal a memory of Young Edie, the belle of East Hampton in her party dress, up in the attic packing a suitcase following the break-up of her engagement. Edie watches her, trying to distinguish the line between the past and the present. Young Edie and Old Edith intone together.)

EDIE and EDITH

Ah–ah–ah–ah–ah . . .

EDIE

Yesterday's dreams,
A faded bouquet.
Roses that died on the vine.
Yesterday seems
More real than today.
It's difficult drawing the line . . .

EDITH

Only a rose . . .
Just a memory divine
Of love,
When sweet youth
Was mine . . .

(The lights fade on Young Edie as she wraps a scrap around her head . . . and flees.)

My season ended
A long time ago . . .
But no one took the party tent down.
The pink paper lanterns
Still twinkle in place.
My young navy hero,
His tender embrace.
That sapphire blue ocean . . .
Oh, how can I face
Another winter in a summer town?
Oh God . . .
Oh God . . .
My God . . .

. . . Ended
A long time ago
All alone now . . .

(Church bells toll in the distance. As Edie stands mute and silent, from upstairs, we hear the familiar cry of Edith calling through the window for Edie.)

EDITH

Edie! What have you done? Where have you gone? I'm all alone!

(The call cuts through Edie like a knife, but she does her damnedest to ignore it.)

(Again, Edith brays.)

Edie! The radio; it's gone dead. The batteries, I think!

(Edie shudders in the evening air. Edith cries out a third time in the growing dark.)

Edie! I'm starving! I want my supper, that's all. I can't . . . ! It won't . . . ! God help me, I can't open the goddamn can! *EDIIIIIIEEE!*

(Edie stands, immobilized, a tiny figure in the great, looming shadow of Grey Gardens. A sigh of resignation, and then . . .)

EDIE

Coming, Mother darling!

(Edie turns and goes back up the path, back through the front door of the house. She leaves the suitcase at the base of the staircase and trudges upstairs to . . .)

SCENE 2—9: EDITH'S BEDROOM

(Edie enters Edith's bedroom.)

EDIE

Honestly. What do you want to do? Wake the neighborhood?

(Edith regards Edie with more gratitude than she could ever express.)

EDITH

Oh, Edie! Wouldn't you like a cup of soup? Wouldn't a cup of soup right now be the most extraordinary thing?

EDIE

Mother, I—

EDITH

With some oyster crackers? Wouldn't it be too divine? Have a cup of soup with your mother, won't you?

(But Edie doesn't answer. Instead, she notices the old record player, standing mute. She crosses to it. With great delicacy, she lifts the lid. Still sitting on it, the record of "Will You," bearing her nasty scratch. She lifts it, turns the record over, and replaces it on the player. She drops the arm.)

(Reprise: "THE GIRL WHO HAS EVERYTHING")

RECORD

She is the girl
Who has everything.
She has the world on a string.
Dancing wherever
Her fancy may please,
Light as a breeze
Brushing the willow trees . . .

EDIE

(turns to her mother)

Which would you like, Mother darling? The cream of tomato or the bisque? You want the bisque?

EDITH

(with magnanimity)

You choose.

RECORD

Cheers to the girl
Who has everything.
Here's to her moment sublime . . .

(Edie obliges, slipping off her coat and laying it on the bed so she can prepare a bowl of soup for her mother. She fetches a can and peers out the window. The great, shuttered eaves and weathered shingles of Grey Gardens close around her.)